A STETHOSCOPE
FOR THE BRAIN

A STETHOSCOPE FOR THE BRAIN

PREVENTIVE APPROACHES TO PROTECT THE MIND

AYAN S. MANDAL

NEW DEGREE PRESS

COPYRIGHT © 2022 AYAN S. MANDAL

A STETHOSCOPE FOR THE BRAIN
Preventive Approaches to Protect the Mind

ISBN   979-8-88504-538-4   *Paperback*
            979-8-88504-864-4   *Kindle Ebook*
            979-8-88504-654-1   *Ebook*

To my family,

None of this is possible without your support

To patients and their families,

I hope this can be of service

CONTENTS

"Those who see inaction in action, and action in inaction, are truly wise amongst humans."

—BHAGAVAD GITA

INTRODUCTION

Between the pool and the beer cooler on a fateful Fourth of July weekend, I had one of those conversations you come to realize, in retrospect, changed everything. I was talking to another college student named Mike, who patiently listened as I explained my lack of a unifying passion. The summer between my freshman and sophomore years of college was punctuated by an identity crisis that I was struggling to resolve. I liked science, but I was truly curious about people, a topic that seemed divorced from the molecules and cells I was studying in my chemistry and biology classes.

Hearing my dilemma, Mike suggested I pick up *The Man Who Mistook His Wife for a Hat* by Oliver Sacks. "He's a doctor," Mike explained, "whose patients have strange problems with their brains." I read the book in a day. Sacks described his patients in a way that embraced their full humanity, despite their uncanny circumstances. He managed to articulate the science of his patients' illnesses with as much thoughtfulness as the personal details that make each individual unique.

This connection between science and people was exactly what I was craving. For example, the man who mistook his wife for a hat was not simply a patient with problems recognizing objects and faces. He was a musician who understood the world through sounds and tunes in the absence of reliable visual cues. I was hooked. I needed to learn more about neurology, the medical discipline responsible for treating people with brain disorders.

While exploring my interest in medicine, I began to understand how common and debilitating brain disorders truly were. Shadowing doctors in the neurology wards, I was most affected by patients with Alzheimer's disease, who struggled to recognize their closest relatives. It took me a few weeks to figure out why they seemed eerily familiar to me until I realized they reminded me of my grandfather.

"He gets treatment for his diabetes. He gets treatment for his blood pressure. Why can't he get treatment for these memory problems? This is what gives us the most stress!" I remembered my father's frustration as he watched his personal hero descend into profound confusion, repeating the same conversations and failing to recognize his own grandchildren. A doctor himself, my father struggled with the fact medicine had very little to offer for his own parent.

In the past, neurology has pejoratively been called a *diagnose and adios* specialty. In other words, the only service a clinician could deliver to a patient with a brain disease was to identify the problem and predict its course. This reputation is quickly changing as scientists churn out new therapies for brain disorders like epilepsy and multiple sclerosis. However, not every brain disease has an effective treatment. It remains hard to feel hopeful as a loved one battles dementia, with too few tools in our arsenal to tackle these devastating conditions.

Why has it been so hard to find good treatments for these disorders? One key reason has to do with the brain's resilience. This incredible organ can withstand substantial damage before a person shows any signs of mental decline. While this feature protects many individuals from cognitive problems, it also means a significant amount of damage is present by the time a person starts to exhibit the signs and symptoms of a brain disorder. Like a house on fire, it is exceedingly difficult to stop a disaster if the response is too late.

Perhaps we need a new approach altogether. It turns out other branches of medicine have confronted a similar problem to what neurology is currently facing. Many cancers and infectious diseases are extremely difficult to treat once a patient arrives at the hospital. While new treatments have played a key role, the doctors in these fields have been able to save countless lives by taking a preventive approach.

Here are just a few examples of how preventive medicine has already revolutionized healthcare. People at risk of breast or colon cancer undergo routine screenings so doctors can remove potential tumors before they become malignant and spread throughout the body. Public health campaigns have discouraged smoking among young people, causing lung cancer rates to plummet. Rigorous sanitation protocols filter out infectious microbes from our drinking water, virtually eliminating cholera from developed countries.

An especially poignant example of the potential behind preventive approaches concerns the COVID-19 pandemic. Millions of lives worldwide were saved during the pandemic, not by the bounties of COVID-19 drugs that have shown varying levels of efficacy, but rather from the handful of vaccines that prevent serious illness. The lesson is clear. We can save some lives by developing new therapies against devastating illnesses. We can save so many more lives by finding new strategies to prevent people from getting extremely sick in the first place.

The metaphor that inspires the book's title—*A Stethoscope for the Brain*—is drawn from a miracle that occurs every day in doctors' offices across the world. You have likely participated in this miracle recently. A physician takes out a blood pressure cuff and a stethoscope, straps the cuff around your arm, inflates the cuff, and listens for your pulse to emerge and vanish as the pressure slowly releases. By noting the pressure values at which your pulse appeared and disappeared, your physician can tell you your risk of having a heart attack in the future and can prescribe medications to help reduce that risk.

Blood pressure measurements are taken for granted because they are so common and so easy to get. But it is exactly these qualities that make this tool a miracle.

Stethoscopes and blood pressure cuffs are cheap and therefore scalable to serve populations worldwide. They are also reliable and precise for monitoring a person's risk of adverse cardiac events. Most importantly, the results of a blood pressure measurement are actionable. If you have high blood pressure, you can change your diet or take medications that lower your risk of a heart attack.

Contrast our ability to monitor and reduce the risk of heart attacks with our current options for Alzheimer's disease. Our options are limited to supportive care after patients have already developed symptoms. It is as if we couldn't intervene on a patient with high blood pressure until after they had already suffered a heart attack. By the time a patient appears at a clinic with memory problems, a significant amount of brain damage has already occurred. Not only are we limited in our ability to screen patients at risk for Alzheimer's disease, but we also lack treatment options that could steer a person toward better brain health even if we knew their risk.

Can neurology mimic the successes of other fields of medicine that have implemented preventive strategies to curb serious diseases? This book intends to explore this idea by outlining current research directions and patient stories that underscore the potential of proactively tackling brain disorders. Maladies of the brain are triggered by a diversity of root causes, and so each chapter highlights a distinct approach for a distinct disease. Some disorders, like multiple sclerosis, could potentially be prevented by vaccines against an infectious agent that appears to cause the illness. Other conditions, like Alzheimer's disease, could be alleviated by public health approaches encouraging social habits, which appear to decrease the risk of dementia.

It has never been more important to discover a better approach to brain health. The other day, I was scrolling through Facebook when I found a picture of my nephew, Nehru, enjoying a bottle of milk fed to him by his great-grandparents (names and details of friends and family have been altered throughout the book). I couldn't help but feel a bit jealous. I barely had the opportunity to meet my parents' parents—my great-grandparents had passed well before I was alive. While anecdotal, the difference between Nehru and me speaks to a larger, epidemiological fact: we are an aging population.

Because of the public health successes over the last few decades, people are living longer than ever before. It is indubitably fortunate that Nehru could meet his great-grandparents, but this shift in the population's demographics nevertheless has consequences.

A major consequence is a large projected uptick in the prevalence of brain diseases, which often increase drastically in risk as one ages. In addition to the personal toll these conditions place on patients and families, we must also consider the economic costs. Dementia currently draws a large segment of the United States' healthcare resources, a proportion that will only grow as life expectancy continues to increase. To prepare for a future where virtually every person will know someone at risk of a brain disorder, we need to be proactive.

This book is for anyone who wants to learn more about common neurological disorders and their prevention. Tackling brain disease in a proactive manner is an interdisciplinary problem, requiring contributions from disparate fields, including neuroscience, behavioral economics, public health, and advocacy. Not only do we need new technologies to detect brain disease earlier, but we also need accessible healthcare systems that allow patients to undergo screening and treatment to realize the vision in this book. Most importantly, we need the medical community, including patients and their families, to rally around strategies to keep everyone safer from brain disease.

Oliver Sacks described a neurology that drew a generation of scientists and doctors to study the brain, including myself. The collective efforts of neurologists like him have given us crucial insights into how the brain works. It is no longer enough, however, to simply describe the diseases of the brain and watch them get worse. As brain disorders grow increasingly common in an aging population, it will be as important as ever to have effective strategies to reduce their burden on patients, their families, and society.

CHAPTER 1.

HOW TO SAVE A BRAIN

Digging into the lower calf of an ex-Marine who donated his body for science, I hold the deep peroneal nerve. This nerve branches from the common peroneal nerve descending from the back of the leg, from where it dives deep, true to its name, to innervate front-facing muscles around the shin. The deep peroneal nerve controls the muscles involved in foot dorsiflexion—that is, the action of raising the front part of the foot to the sky, so only the heel touches the ground.

Or at least, this is what I gathered from my instructor, a seasoned surgeon who has been operating on broken bones since the Reagan administration. It is my third month of medical school, and I am starting to get what my father meant when he said digesting the information you learn during the first year is like "drinking out of a firehose." To keep up with the material, I think of silly mnemonics to help me recall certain associations—"the deep peroneal nerve does dorsiflexion, which lets you walk like a duck."

I take a break from the anatomy lab's pickle jar smell to consider the organization of the nervous system, a topic closer to my heart. When dissecting the tattooed leg of the cadaver given to me, trying my best to honor the body while memorizing its anatomy, I am studying the peripheral nervous system.

The peripheral nervous system is comprised of the nerves outside the brain and spinal cord, which sense the outside environment and orchestrate the movements of muscles. This consortium of nerves both receives signals from and sends signals to the central nervous system, which is comprised of the spinal cord and brain. The most human abilities, including thought, decision-making, and consciousness, are housed in the central nervous system, or more precisely, in the brain.

For the peripheral nerves outside of the brain that control the movements of muscles, we can say the nerve *does* a certain action without any ambiguity. The deep peroneal nerve *does* dorsiflexion. If this nerve is damaged, dorsiflexion is not possible. Does the same direct association between singular anatomical structures and cognitive abilities still apply when considering regions within the brain? In the same way we have peripheral nerves that control the flexing of the wrist or the kicking of the foot, do we also have dedicated brain structures responsible for language or memory?

Perhaps no person was more consequential for this debate than a nineteenth-century French man named Louis Victor Leborgne. Leborgne spent his final twenty-one years in a hospital for the mentally ill, to which he was admitted with a peculiar problem. His vocabulary was limited to just one syllable: *Tan.*

Since he lacked a more complex speech, Leborgne would communicate by articulating this syllable with varying intonations while demonstrating his needs with hand gestures. To signal he was thirsty, he likely needed to mime out the action of drinking a glass of water after grabbing a nurse's attention with a loud "Tan!"

Despite his admission to a hospital for the mentally ill, Leborgne retained all of the cognitive abilities of a healthy individual—except for language, of course. His brain injury—whatever it turned out to be—had zapped his ability to speak but spared his memory, attention, and intellect, all abilities that contribute to language.

Given a watch missing the second hand, Leborgne could indicate where the hand should be, demonstrating his ability to perceive the passage of time (Mohammed et al., 2018). He knew exactly how long he had been in the hospital. The mere existence of Leborgne posed major issues for popular theories of the brain, where mental functions like language were thought to be interdependent with other basic functions.

In particular, Leborgne's existence posed issues for Louis Pierre Gratiolet. A neuroanatomist by training, Gratiolet was a founding member of the Anthropology Society of Paris. This society, coincidentally founded the same year as the publication of Charles Darwin's *The Origin of*

Species in 1859, reflected a transitional state in Western European thought.

Many Parisian intellectuals maintained the metaphysical claims of their grandfathers, believing in a separation between mind, body, and soul. Yet they were starting to consider how the findings of science may question certain spiritual claims. For example, a major topic of debate in the society concerned the association between head size and intelligence, a relationship that could support the material basis of mental functions if proved legitimate.

It was Gratiolet's mission to refute arguments claiming properties of the brain directly contribute to mental function. Gratiolet subscribed to a somewhat mystical theory wherein all parts of the brain, in unity, were responsible for complex cognitive abilities, such as language and memory. He would poke holes in the studies that claimed a relationship between head size and intelligence, which often relied on human skull remains of poor quality (Sondhaus and Finger, 1988).

Perhaps surprising for a neuroanatomist, Gratiolet maintained the role of a Soul, untethered to matter, in conducting the most critical activities of a person (Lorch, 2011). Little did he know that miles away from his meetings rested a man in a hospital bed whose clinical profile would convince the following generations of scholars that he was wrong.

Gratiolet and Leborgne's stories would cross paths thanks to a surgeon named Paul Broca. Broca was another founding member of the Anthropology Society of Paris. His views generally contradicted those of Gratiolet. He bought into the association between intelligence and brain size. He was also open to the ideas of his mentor, the physician Ernest Auburtin, who insisted that the frontal lobes of the brain conduct language function.

Years of clinical practice had introduced Aubertin to scores of patients who had endured strokes that stole their ability to speak, impressing upon him the idea that focal brain damage can disrupt mental function. But it wasn't until Broca treated his own patient experiencing profound language impairments that he was fully convinced of the essential role of brain for behavior.

Ten years into his hospital admission, Leborgne's condition began to deteriorate. He started to lose control over the right half of his body and developed a putrid infection of his leg. The doctors called Broca in to amputate the leg. Interviewing Leborgne, his family, and other doctors to obtain a detailed medical history, Broca was struck by the specificity of Leborgne's speech deficit.

Other patients of his had speech problems, but they were often the result of paralysis or severe intellectual disability. Leborgne, on the other hand, had problems speaking, but all other cognitive domains that Broca could test were normal. Broca found Leborgne's presentation so intriguing he designated it with its own name, *aphemie*, or loss of articulated speech. This condition is now known as aphasia, a general language deficit and a common consequence of strokes that injure the left hemisphere, or half, of the brain.

After Leborgne passed away, Broca was eager to conduct the autopsy. He wanted to know what type of injury was responsible for aphemie. Was it a diffuse injury with a broad impact on the whole brain, as would be predicted by Gratiolet? Or was it a focal injury affecting one specific region of the brain that reflects the part responsible for speech?

A thorough dissection was not necessary to answer this question definitively. Broca spotted a clear, singular injury on the surface of Leborgne's lateral frontal lobe, a region of the brain now commonly referred to as *Broca's area*. Broca presented Leborgne's brain to the Anthropology Society the next day, and the audience was quickly convinced. Gratiolet was wrong. Auburtin and Broca were validated.

* * *

In most medical textbooks, the story ends here. Within these gratified tomes that form the basis of modern healing, you will find colored areas of the brain corresponding to Broca's area, the *speech center*, and also Wernicke's area, a region discovered later that is involved in speech comprehension.

Medical students learn about the brain the same way they learn about the peripheral nerves—just as the deep peroneal nerve *does* dorsiflexion, Broca's area *does* speech. Could it really be so simple? Like most things in science, the truth is more complicated, and the thinking on this issue did not end in 1880 after Paul Broca passed away.

Several recent developments in the field of language neuroscience have challenged the notion that Broca's area is critical for speech production. First, note that Broca could not fully examine Leborgne's injury since he insisted on preserving the brain for future research. This decision proved critically prescient, as the development of new imaging technologies like magnetic resonance imaging (MRI) have allowed scientists to reexamine Leborgne's brain in greater detail.

These modern investigations have revealed that Leborgne's brain damage was not exclusive to Broca's area (Dronkers et al., 2007). The cuts to his brain extended deeper, affecting white matter tracts in the frontal lobe. We can think of white matter tracts as the highways of the brain, which allow communication between distant brain regions.

If Broca's area and the underlying white matter were both affected in Leborgne's injury, how can we decide which was responsible for his inability to produce speech? It is impossible without more data. In the centuries following Broca's death, it has been extremely difficult to tease apart the contribution of Broca's area versus frontal white matter to speech deficits. Most strokes will inevitably implicate both regions, given their close proximity. Only recently has an answer emerged. By studying over one hundred individuals with varying degrees of damage to Broca's area, investigators at the University College London determined that frontal white matter plays a more crucial role in long-term speech outcomes (Gajardo-Villal et al., 2021).

These findings demonstrate that the connections between regions, as opposed to each region in isolation, are often responsible for cognitive functions like language. The newer science partially vindicates Gratiolet's idea of widespread brain regions working in unity across a network. While connection-based models of brain function were considered abstract and untestable in the past, the technology has now emerged to identify brain networks and rigorously assess their role in cognitive ability.

Quick facts are drilled into my head while studying for medical school exams—"deep peroneal nerve does dorsiflexion, which helps you walk like a duck." But the truth is we can ascribe no function to one structure alone. The deep peroneal nerve connects with the spinal cord, where it receives necessary signals from upper motor neurons that live in the brain. Those upper motor neurons communicate with other neuronal networks that decide whether dorsiflexion is appropriate. Any injury along this pathway will impair your ability to walk like a duck.

The practice of deciphering brain function by investigating brain injuries has been critical in the history of neuroscience. Just as medical students today learn about the body by examining donated cadavers, so did the physicians of the past centuries, correlating abnormalities they found at autopsy with the syndromes their patients displayed during life. As shown by the recent findings from the researchers at University College London, we still use this approach to refine our predictions of brain function. However, what is the benefit to the patient with aphasia, who walks into the hospital with a sudden inability to speak if we know the precise location of the injury causing their deficit?

* * *

To make the leap from simply knowing about the brain to actually treating brain disorders, we need to focus on what *causes* these conditions instead of only studying their consequences. What causes aphasia?

Language ability can be disturbed by several types of injuries, including head trauma and neurodegeneration, but by far, the most common cause of aphasia is a stroke. A stroke results from a sudden loss of blood flow to a particular brain region due to either a blood clot or a brain bleed. The symptoms of a stroke will vary depending on the brain region affected. Aphasia reflects just one of a wide range of problems that can be initiated by a stroke.

After a stroke, patients will typically improve over the next few months as their brain starts to rewire in order to compensate for the damage. Rehabilitation with physical therapists and spoken language pathologists is crucial in facilitating this recovery. Despite the best efforts of the patient and their care team, however, recovery can sometimes be limited for patients who suffered a very large stroke.

The most important strategy we can take is to prevent strokes from happening in the first place. All of the preventive measures that work against heart attack also apply for stroke prevention—meaning keeping one's blood pressure in check, exercising regularly, and eating healthy food. But one can do all of the right things and, because of a combination of genetics and bad luck, still suffer from a stroke. What can a person do to limit the damage of a stroke and ensure a fast, lasting recovery?

"Time is brain," reads a sign I walk past every day on my way to the medical school. If you peer a bit closer, you can read an explanation: "treatment within three hours of a stroke improves chances of recovery with little or no disability." This means if you see a person with sudden numbness or weakness in one half of their body, slurred speech, impaired balance, or a drooping face, you will want to rush them to a hospital as soon as possible in case they are suffering from a stroke.

In the days of Paul Broca, how quickly a stroke patient arrived at the hospital would not have mattered much. There wasn't much the doctors could have done about it. Physicians then were just beginning to learn that language problems like those seen in Leborgne could be caused by damage to blood vessels. Armed with a detailed understanding of the types of injuries behind strokes, we now have strategies to stop them in their tracks.

For strokes caused by blood clots, patients can receive a medication that busts these clots, saving critical brain tissue that otherwise could have died from a lack of oxygen. However, this medication will only help if administered to a patient within a few hours after the onset of symptoms. In some situations, a doctor can perform a procedure called a thrombectomy to surgically remove the clot using a gadget that looks like a fishing net. This operation involves fitting a tube in from the groin and threading it through a network of blood vessels, all the way up to the brain to retrieve the clot.

The quicker an anticlotting treatment is given, the more brain tissue that is saved—thus prompting the slogan *time is brain*. While large strokes are difficult to recover from, the brain can work around a smaller injury, increasing the likelihood of avoiding severe impairment.

The new neurology would not exist without the old neurology. The relationship that Broca described between frontal lobe injuries and language difficulties, albeit imperfect, still plays a critical role in the early identification of a stroke. The insights gained by early neurologists, who meticulously classified and described brain diseases, will remain crucial as we develop new treatments for these disorders. The story behind anticlotting treatments for stroke also suggests a way forward for the treatment of other brain diseases.

The recipe for optimal stroke treatment is simple: identify early, then treat early. Could the same recipe work for other disorders?

CHAPTER 2

SIX DEGREES OF NEURAL CONNECTION

At ten past six, in the cafe where he did all his writing, Frigyes Karinthy heard the first train. The sound of steam pressing the air took him back to his childhood, the last time he had seen a train on the hilly streets of Budapest. But isn't that odd? All the trains built in Budapest had been electric since he turned seven. It wasn't until the fourth train buzzed by that he realized there were no trains, or at least none that anyone else around him could appreciate. The train was unique to his consciousness—he was hallucinating.

Born into a bourgeois Hungarian society in 1887, Frigyes Karinthy was a playwright famous within his community for his short stories (Karinthy, 1939). He was a character within a world increasingly defined by vast social connections, as advanced methods of travel and communication had eliminated physical distance as a barrier to friendship. In his most famous short story, titled "Chain-Links," he described the growing connectedness of the world, postulating that no more than five social links separated any two human beings.

As you may guess, "Chain-Links" introduced concepts that have since proliferated throughout social science and popular culture. If you have ever remarked, "It's a small world!" after bumping into a college friend in Marrakesh or traced the few degrees of separation between your favorite actor and Kevin Bacon, you have Karinthy to thank for the language you use to describe these observations.

Literary accomplishments aside, Karinthy had a problem. Punctually, at seven o'clock every evening, the trains continued to run for him but no one else. He elected to see several specialists regarding his hallucinations—an ear doctor, a psychoanalyst, a general physician—but none could provide a satisfying explanation.

And his problems were increasing in number. Karinthy had started having bad headaches. He had also endured an intense episode of nausea and vomiting that he couldn't trace back to anything he had eaten. Something was wrong, and he needed to get to the bottom of it.

After months of scrambling between four different doctors, it was Karinthy himself, a medical school dropout, who first arrived at the correct diagnosis. He decided to confide his fears to his wife, Aranka, also a physician.

"Aranka, I've got a tumor on the brain."

"You don't say so! A man of your age, too. You ought to be ashamed of yourself. You talk like a first-year medical student."

Karinthy's wife was referring to the tendency of medical students to identify with the myriad of symptoms they learn are diagnostic for various diseases. I've fallen prey to this behavior as well when I woke up in the middle of the night in sweats thinking I contracted tuberculosis when really I had just forgotten to turn on the air conditioner.

Karinthy's sudden suspicion arose after visiting the wards with his wife and encountering a patient with a brain tumor, whose furrowed eyebrows and look of dread reminded him of what he saw every day in the mirror.

Revealing this insight to his wife, she retorted:

"Well, let me give you a lesson for the future. There are three standard symptoms for diagnosing a tumor on the brain—headaches, retching with giddiness, and papillitis."

"Well, the headaches and the retching I've had already. Only I didn't want to say anything about it. And as for the pap—papil—What did you call it?"

Papillitis is a term that refers to damage to the papilla, which is a structure in the back of the eye. When there is increased pressure within the skull due to a brain tumor or some other mass, the brain pushes into the eye—the path of least resistance. This pressure compresses the blood vessels in the papilla, which is a useful sign a physician can detect using an ophthalmoscope.

Advances in brain imaging have made the diagnosis of a brain tumor more straightforward in the modern-day. Your physician can order an MRI scan if they suspect a brain tumor. However, this technology was not available in the early twentieth century, so physicians made this diagnosis exactly how Aranka describes, by examining the eye for a sign of increased pressure within the skull.

Despite his wife's assurances, Karinthy decided to see his ophthalmologist, hoping to clear his mind of the concern he harbored about this deadly condition. Directing a beam of light into his eye, the ophthalmologist discovered papillitis, clear and unfortunate evidence supporting Karinthy's suspicion.

From a series of neurological exams, X-rays, and other diagnostic tests, Karinthy's physicians eventually converged on the opinion that he indeed suffered from a brain tumor. Likely a meningioma was affecting the cerebellum, a densely packed wormlike structure in the back of the brain. Given the importance of the cerebellum for coordination, Karinthy's physicians may have noticed impairments in his sense of balance, failing the same tests you might ask someone whom you suspect is too drunk to perform.

Generally, there are three main types of brain tumors an adult may have: a glioma, a brain metastasis, or a meningioma. Of these, meningiomas have the most favorable clinical outcome. These tumors form out of the brain's outer membrane and exert external pressure that can lead to various problems that are generally not life-threatening, like worsening vision.

However, neither Karinthy nor his physicians fully understood the distinction between the outcomes of meningiomas versus the other, more lethal types of brain tumors. On one occasion, a physician informed him he would soon suffer from serious mental deterioration after examining his papilla, a prediction that turned out to be inaccurate.

In almost all cases, brain tumors are treated surgically by removing the mass from the brain. For meningiomas, surgical removal of the tumor is usually curative. Karinthy's headaches and hallucinations resolved after a Swedish neurosurgeon removed his tumor. However, surgical removal is not curative for other types of brain tumors, such as gliomas, which form from the brain's supporting cells. These tumors infiltrate the brain diffusely, so removing the tumor mass does not eliminate all of the cancer. As a result, these types of brain tumors are extremely difficult to treat and almost always lead to death.

Could our ability to treat brain tumors improve if approached proactively? We know early diagnosis can vastly improve outcomes for other types of cancer. And indeed, for brain metastases—tumors that begin somewhere else in the body and then travel to the brain—treating the cancer before it metastasizes could prevent the problem altogether. However, for tumors that originate in the brain, like gliomas, there is unfortunately no good evidence that treating these cancers early improves outcomes for patients.

Unlike other malignancies such as lung cancer, there are very few predictive risk factors for brain tumors. That means that in most cases, acquiring a brain tumor is a random event unrelated to genes inherited from family or lifestyle factors like smoking. The only known risk factor for brain tumors is exposure to radiation, which highlights the importance of ridding radioactive materials from our environment. But the bottom-line is that brain tumors are almost impossible to predict, and even if we could predict them, intervening early will not necessarily lead to better outcomes.

In the absence of any good way to prevent brain tumors, we must ask whether we can treat these malignancies proactively after diagnosis. And here's where Frigyes Karinthy's insights regarding social connectedness become relevant in the treatment of brain tumors. The network principles he introduced to the world in his short story "Chain-Links" may one day be used to plan treatments that thwart brain tumors before they reappear.

* * *

London's Heathrow Airport is a familiar destination to me. I attended graduate school in the United Kingdom, and before that, I've almost always had a layover there on my way to visit family in India. Heathrow is an extremely busy site since it hosts many connecting flights to help travelers get between two places where there may not be any direct journey. In this way, international air travel mirrors the patterns of social networks. Just as fewer than six degrees of separation exist between Kevin Bacon and me, one can transit from Canada to Lithuania in only a couple of flights, likely by way of Heathrow Airport.

Like air travel, the human brain is also a densely interconnected system. Neuroscientists have described the brain as a *small world network*, where any two brain regions can communicate with ease, utilizing only a few connections (Bassett and Bullmore, 2006). While such efficiency is crucial for all of the immensely complicated things that human brains can do, like planning a European vacation, it also makes the brain vulnerable to diseases that exploit its connectivity.

It turns out that some brain pathologies, including tumors, can spread widely by traveling along brain networks. Brain tumor cells can travel along blood vessels as well as white matter pathways, the highways of neural connections between distant brain regions. Therefore, while it may seem from a brain scan that a tumor is in a single location, cells from that tumor may have branched off and traveled along these connections to sprout in several other areas of the brain.

Another example from the early twentieth century illustrates how difficult diffuse gliomas are to treat. The legacy of William Halsted lingered over surgical oncology in those days. Dr. Halsted was a founding member of the Johns Hopkins Hospital who trained legions of surgeons to approach cancer aggressively (Mukherjee, 2011). He famously championed the radical mastectomy for breast cancer, a surgery removing the whole breast, underlying chest muscles, and lymph nodes. Later generations proved this procedure futile if the cancer had already metastasized. Still, the neurosurgeon Walter Dandy attempted a similar approach to glioma, removing the entire half of the brain in which the tumor lived (Dandy, 1928). Even this proved futile, as the tumor mass would reappear in the opposite hemisphere just months later, presumably having traveled across the connections between both halves of the brain.

Current therapeutic strategies against brain tumors involve surgical removal of the tumor mass and radiation targeted at the surrounding tissue to destroy any lingering tumor cells. But these current approaches do not account for the fact the tumor will inevitably reappear at a different site. How can we design therapies that prevent the tumor from ever returning?

One encouraging advance from the past couple of decades of research is the unveiling of the human *connectome*, or a wiring diagram of the human brain. The connectome has already led to several clinical insights, including an understanding of why damage to distributed brain locations can lead to the same symptoms, as well as a roadmap for designing personalized therapies for patients with psychiatric illnesses. Research from my dissertation work has indicated that brain tumors spread along the connectome, suggesting this wiring diagram could predict where a tumor might appear next (Mandal et al.,

2020). Such predictions could inform preemptive treatments for brain tumors, targeting brain regions that might not seem to harbor tumor cells yet but are likely to develop a tumor soon.

The notion of targeting a brain region that looks healthy, but might be cancerous, brings up a crucial dilemma in the search for proactive strategies against brain diseases. Such preemptive strategies might have side effects, such as cognitive issues a patient might experience after targeting a healthy brain. How do we do our best to comprehensively eliminate a cancer, while minimizing collateral damage to the body? This question is universal in the world of oncology.

The ideal treatment for any cancer, especially brain cancer, would kill only the tumor cells and not touch any healthy cells. Current treatments for cancer, like chemotherapy, disproportionately eliminate tumor cells but also affect healthy cells, leading to bad side effects. Where might a magic bullet be found, a therapy that comprehensively and selectively eliminates cancer? A good place to start is to consider the body's intrinsic reaction to cancer—the immune response.

It is a scary thought, but cancers arise in the body all the time. Most people do not experience the symptoms of their cancer until old age because the body's immune system is able to squash malignancies before they cause any problems. The cancers that do cause clinical problems are typically those that have evolved mechanisms to evade the immune system.

For instance, a cancer cell can express a signal that diverts the immune system, making it look the other way. Such a cell can survive, thrive unperturbed, and ultimately proliferate into a tumor. If you turn on the TV and find an ad for a new cancer therapy, the odds are that it is a drug that has taken advantage of this insight. For example, a popular drug called Keytruda works by blocking the *Don't Eat Me!* signal sometimes expressed by cancer cells, thus recruiting the immune system to kill the tumor.

Since immune cells can effectively thwart cancer, some scientists have attempted to design their own immune cells that specifically attack tumors and infuse these into patients as a therapy. These specially engineered cells are called chimeric antigen receptor T cells or CAR-T cells for short. They are already being used to treat some cancers, most notably leukemia.

In theory, CAR-T cells could be a very effective option for infiltrative brain tumors since they would patrol the brain and eliminate lingering cancer cells even if they have traveled far from the initial tumor mass. A few clinical trials testing the effectiveness of CAR-T cells for gliomas have had initial promising results (Majner et al., 2022), yet many challenges remain. For example, the same mechanisms by which cancers evade the body's immune system also work against the CAR-T cells, so we need to design therapies that can stay one step ahead.

The options for treating brain cancer are dizzying—surgery, chemotherapy, radiation, immunotherapy. Is one of these approaches better than the rest? The truth is the best treatment regimens will likely combine multiple modalities since cancers can develop resistance to any single therapy. Consider the following example. Let's say you have discovered a new chemotherapy that kills 99.9 percent of the cells in a tumor. While this drug may appear extremely effective at eliminating the cancer, a new tumor that is resistant to the therapy can still sprout from the 0.1 percent of surviving cells. The best way to prevent this from happening is to combine several therapies to eliminate as much of the tumor as possible.

While we have made several strides in our ability to treat brain tumors since Karinthy's diagnosis in the early twentieth century, survival rates among patients with gliomas have remained stagnantly grim over the past twenty years. Despite decades of research, there hasn't yet been a breakthrough in our search for a cure for these deadly conditions. However, we have learned why our therapies often fail, and it has a lot to do with Karinthy's concept of *six degrees of separation*. Just as our global society can be described as a small world, so too can the human brain, as the brain's connectedness makes it easy for tumors to spread. The good news is that researchers are developing new therapies which address the fact that cancers can infiltrate along brain networks. The ultimate goal is to stay one step ahead of brain tumors, an endeavor that should get easier once we can predict which paths they will take.

CHAPTER 3

BEFORE THE FALL

It was not the fall that triggered a deep concern and philosophical reconsideration for Michael. Having lived with Parkinson's disease for three decades, awkward encounters with the ground were not so unusual for him. Rather, it was his body's reaction to the fall, the lack of a response from his left arm as he shifted his weight to the side—that's what got him worried.

He fears that he broke his arm, a suspicion that turns out to be accurate (Fox, 2020). Yet this injury is relatively minor compared to his other medical problems, which include a neurodegenerative disease and a tumor that threatens his spinal cord.

What really worries Michael is not the broken arm itself but what the precipitating fall represents—the possibility that he may have been wrong when he told himself and others to look on the bright side, to find the silver lining, to make lemonade out of lemons when a doctor discloses terrible news to you and your family.

"I had this crisis of conscience," said Michael in a 2020 interview with the *New York Times.* "I thought, 'what have I been telling people?' I tell people it's all going to be okay—and it might suck!"

People like Michael try to find the silver lining in every challenging situation, but sometimes this is impossible. Not every obstacle will emerge with a critical lesson that makes the struggle worthwhile. Nevertheless, Michael's life is a testament to the power of optimism in medicine and how daring to dream of a better future, even if naively imagined, can provide a roadmap to improving the lives of millions.

Our Michael, of course, is the inimitable Michael J. Fox, the famed actor in *Back to the Future* and *Family Ties.* That same actor faced down one of the most terrifying medical diagnoses and emerged as an even greater star. It seemed to start in his late twenties when he noticed his finger twitching during a film shoot in Florida. A short time later, he reported his symptoms to a neurologist, and an exam revealed he had Parkinson's disease.

The cause of Parkinson's disease is a slow yet persistent degeneration of neurons that produce a chemical called dopamine in the basal ganglia, a circuit of brain structures tasked with initiating and stopping movement. Patients with Parkinson's disease have difficulty walking and talking because of this brain damage, a problem treated by medications that increase the brain's supply of dopamine. An exam like the one that Michael's neurologist performed will demonstrate slow movements, rigid limbs, a resting tremor, and a shuffling gait.

While Michael is comfortable speaking publicly about his condition now, it wasn't always that way. Before his diagnosis, Michael was already handling the tricky transition from a career as a child actor to an adult star. Parkinson's was an additional stress and one he could hide for several years because of the slow progression of the disease. Since the symptoms were minor initially, it was possible for Michael to remain in denial of the eventual outcomes of the condition (Freeman, 2020). "I had a twitching problem and a sore shoulder. [The doctors] said, 'You won't be able to work in a few years,' and I'm thinking, 'From this?'"

Eventually, his symptoms grew more apparent, making it harder to keep his condition a secret. The trembling of his arm became so bad that he asked his limousine driver to circle the block three times before dropping him off at the 1998 Golden Globe Awards, waiting for the tremors to stop before he set foot on the red carpet (The Washington Post, 1998). Tragic for an actor defined by physical comedy, his body stopped cooperating with his acting schedule. He found himself punching his own arm before shooting scenes of *Spin City*, begging his limbs to act normal. It became impossible to hide his Parkinson's. He could keep his secret no longer.

Michael went from hiding his disease to becoming the face of Parkinson's in just a few years. He established the Michael J. Fox Foundation in 1998, a fundraising organization that started with a bold goal: "Our deal is to be out of business within ten years."

The foundation has been wildly successful, raising over one billion dollars for Parkinson's disease research. Yet the clear burden that this condition continues to place on the more than one million Americans living with the disease—and their loved ones—clearly demonstrates that the founding goal was much too optimistic (Marras et al., 2018). Why has a cure for Parkinson's disease remained so elusive, despite the substantial financial and intellectual resources devoted to investigating it?

* * *

"I have to show you something," Michael says to his close friends, seeing them for the first time since breaking his arm. He flashes a photo of an X-ray of his broken arm and takes some relief when their eyes widen, understanding what's exactly wrong. Unlike Parkinson's disease, he does not need to explain how this broken arm affects him, what it feels like, or what he can and can't do because of it.

There is no X-ray for the biological mechanisms behind Parkinson's disease. We only have the patient's symptoms. And because the disease process begins decades before the patient starts to exhibit symptoms, candidate therapeutics would be administered far too late to be effective.

That the disease is likely to have progressed significantly before a patient enrolls in a clinical trial is thought to be a major reason why promising treatments aimed at reversing Parkinson's fail to show any benefit. Perhaps our best hope at addressing this problem is to develop better diagnostic methods to catch Parkinson's disease *before* the patient starts to tremor.

A major initiative of the Michael J. Fox Foundation is to identify biomarkers that permit the diagnosis of Parkinson's before symptoms arise. A biomarker is an easily obtained measurement that tracks a patient's risk for developing a given disease. For example, blood pressure is a good biomarker to identify patients at risk for heart disease so they can receive medications to reduce this risk. Through the Parkinson's Progression Markers Initiative, the Michael J. Fox Foundation is testing the validity of potential biomarkers for Parkinson's disease, including brain scans, blood tests, and assays of proteins in the cerebrospinal fluid that coats the brain.

How might a brain scan detect Parkinson's disease? An important hallmark always found at autopsy in patients who have died with Parkinson's is a clump of proteins called a Lewy body. In several neurodegenerative conditions, including Parkinson's disease, Lewy bodies develop inside neurons, causing significant brain damage. Currently, Lewy bodies are only detectable at autopsy. If we could detect them from a brain scan, we would be able to identify the early signs of neurodegeneration and perhaps start treating patients earlier.

Using positron emission tomography (PET), scientists funded by the Michael J. Fox Foundation have made significant strides in developing the technology to take a picture of Parkinson's in those still living with the disease (Michael J. Fox Foundation, 2022). PET is a special imaging technique that uses a radioactive tracer that binds to a molecule of interest and sends out radiation. A scanner can then detect this radiation to locate the molecule.

To find Lewy bodies in the brain, scientists administered one such radioactive tracer into the veins of volunteers with multiple system atrophy, a neurodegenerative condition similar to Parkinson's disease and associated with Lewy bodies. The tracer found its way into the brain, where it glued itself to Lewy bodies in the cerebellum, the brain region most affected by multiple system atrophy. Since the tracer is radioactive, it emits particles that can be detected by the PET scanner, allowing scientists to pinpoint the location of the Lewy bodies. A procedure like this could one day detect Parkinson's before it causes significant problems, when the disease might still be reversible.

Bone fractures and brain diseases may seem like separate issues, but neurology has a lot to learn from how endocrinologists prevent the former. Endocrinologists can screen elderly patients at risk of bone fractures by diagnosing osteoporosis, a condition marked by decreased bone density and bone quality. Your doctor can tell if you have osteoporosis by acquiring special X-ray scans of your bones, from which they can obtain a measure of bone density. They compare this measure of bone density to a range of possible healthy values. If the patient falls below that range, there is a concern for osteoporosis. The doctor might then prescribe medications that preserve bone health and counsel the patient on ways to prevent falls and other accidents.

Ranges of what is considered normal are ubiquitous in medicine. To diagnose iron deficiency, for example, the amount of iron in a patient's blood should fall below a range of healthy values. However, it is not currently possible to tell if a person's brain is "normal" from a brain scan. Reduced brain volume compared to a normal range could be an early sign of neurodegeneration, just as reduced bone density suggests a risk for bone fractures.

To develop normal ranges for brain tissue volumes across the lifespan, researchers at the University of Pennsylvania led by Dr. Aaron Alexander-Bloch established growth charts for the human brain (Bethlehem, Seidlitz, and White et al., 2022). Body growth charts are a commonly used tool among pediatricians in evaluating whether a child is at an appropriate height or weight for someone of their age and biological sex. For example, a malnourished, three-year-old boy might score in the third percentile for weight compared to other three-year-old boys, which could prompt an evaluation for a possible cause of his low score.

By collecting over 100,000 brain scans from across the world, Dr. Alexander-Bloch and his team developed charts that are useful for deriving percentile scores of the brain for individuals of any age. They showed that low percentile scores for brain volume characterized the early stages of Alzheimer's disease. While doctors currently use brain imaging to identify qualitative signs of disease, such as the presence of a stroke or tumor, these brain charts can offer quantitative data in support of a diagnosis. Just as with screening a malnourished child, brain charts could one day help diagnose neurodegenerative conditions like Parkinson's disease earlier, before symptoms arise.

* * *

In addition to the lack of biomarkers, another barrier to finding new treatments for Parkinson's disease is the heterogeneity among patients diagnosed with the condition, illustrated by Michael's own story. Michael was diagnosed at twenty-nine, decades before most people begin to exhibit symptoms of Parkinson's disease. While this early onset clinical presentation shares many of the same features of late-onset Parkinson's disease, it is extremely likely that Michael's condition had a different underlying cause. In other words, Parkinson's disease is merely a term referring to a constellation of symptoms affecting movement, where a range of distinct causes could lead to the same outcome.

This heterogeneity poses a massive problem for clinical trials of drugs intended to reverse a specific underlying disease process in Parkinson's. The disease could be taking a different course for a sizable portion of the enrolled patients. Investigators design clinical trials to combat this heterogeneity by applying strict inclusion criteria. For instance, a trial may limit their scope to individuals above the age of sixty-five without a family history of neurodegenerative disease so that their study population includes only individuals with sporadic, late-onset Parkinson's disease. However, because we are not currently aware of the myriad subtypes of Parkinson's disease, our ability to mitigate heterogeneity in clinical trials is limited.

Two initiatives from the Michael J. Fox Foundation target this obstacle to drug development. The first, which is called *Fox Insight*, aims to characterize the variability of Parkinson's disease by collecting comprehensive histories of over 30,000 individuals with the condition. By tracking the daily experiences, family histories, and medical issues of a large, diverse cohort of Parkinson's patients, researchers can begin to sift through the data to discover possible subtypes of the disease.

Some individuals are invited to participate in genetic testing via the personal genomics company 23AndMe, which could provide insight into the role of genetics in dictating how Parkinson's disease manifests for them. No group of people—not scientists, not doctors, not professors—is more knowledgeable about Parkinson's disease than those living with it. Therefore, the Fox Insight initiative reflects an opportunity to mine this critical expertise to break the condition into meaningful subtypes, improving clinical trial design.

A major obstacle for clinical trials is patient recruitment, especially when the inclusion criteria need to be strict. Another initiative called the Fox Trial Finder efficiently matches patients to clinical trials that fit their diagnoses, demographics, and geographic locations. Clinical trial recruitment is normally decentralized and communicated through word-of-mouth or online advertising. By centralizing the process, it is easier than ever for patients to contribute to the discovery of new drugs to possibly improve the care of future patients afflicted with the same condition. Many patients with severe diseases derive significant satisfaction and a sense of purpose from helping others like them in this way.

Parkinson's disease remains incurable, but there are several reasons to stay hopeful. We are learning how to take pictures of the disease in the brain, which can help us diagnose and start treating the condition earlier. We are also starting to understand better the different subtypes of Parkinson's disease, which will one day help physicians individualize treatment to optimize results. Each of these advances will aid the design of clinical trials to find new drugs to help patients maintain their autonomy in the face of their disease.

"I'd hoped we'd be out of business by now. I thought we'd find a cure—oil and dog hair will fix it, something like that," Michael joked toward the end of his 2020 *New York Times* interview. Curing Parkinson's disease has clearly not been so easy, yet optimism is nevertheless warranted in the fight against this debilitating illness.

Two types of optimism exist. One type of optimism is simply wishful thinking, an assumption that everything will be okay since the alternative is too difficult to confront. This type of optimism can be a helpful short-term coping mechanism, yet it is doomed to shatter once reality sets in. Michael began his journey with naive optimism, but it dimmed as his condition worsened, eventually reaching a breaking point as his humerus bone fractured.

A second type of optimism is obtained with maturity, by seeing both the glass-half-empty and glass-half-full perspectives and choosing to have faith in the latter. This is an informed optimism built off a thorough appreciation of the obstacles yet a persistent drive to jump every hurdle. Oil and dog hair won't cure it, but through the collective effort of patients, doctors, scientists, and philanthropists, a world without Parkinson's disease has become more than just a naively optimistic dream.

CHAPTER 4

HOT HEARTS, COOL HEADS, AND INFLAMED MINDS

Like many intellectual disciplines, the study of biology is traceable to the Greek philosopher Aristotle. A true empiricist, Aristotle relied not on speculation but on dissections of organisms to uncover the principles that govern life. Despite his positive influence on the physical sciences, one glaring error of his stands out:

"And of course, the brain is not responsible for any sensations at all. The correct view [is] that the seat and source of sensation is the region of the heart." (Parts of Animals, translated by A.L. Peck, 1955).

Aristotle was not alone in this now ludicrous position. The Egyptians also hailed the heart as the center of consciousness and preserved it—not the brain—after death (Gross, 1995). One pre-Socratic thinker, Empedocles, taught that blood was the medium of thought, thus implying that cognition depends on cardiac function. On the other hand,

Greek physicians like Hippocrates and Alcmaeon of Cro-
ton noted that the sense organs—eyes, nose, and mouth—
all directly surrounded the brain. Therefore, it would be
most efficient for the brain to receive these senses and
direct actions accordingly.

Aristotle countered that much physical sensation comes
through touch, which can be felt anywhere in the body
receiving blood. So it is actually the centrally located
heart that receives information from every corner of the
human figure. He also noted that the heart responds to
emotion, stops beating when life ends, and is naturally
hot in temperature, a shared characteristic among most
living things. Like most of Aristotle's positions, his argu-
ment for the heart's supremacy was compelling at the
time of his writing, despite the objective inaccuracy of
his overall conclusions.

One must admit that Aristotle's picture of cognition,
though incorrect, is nonetheless poetic. He does not
completely dismiss the brain; rather, he posits that the
brain is responsible for *cooling* the heart. He describes
a homeostasis in which the brain and the heart must
counterbalance one another for proper decision-making.
This line of reasoning aligns with his thoughts on the
golden mean, or the idea that virtue lies in the middle
of two extreme vices—so courage is a virtue, in between
the vices of cowardice and recklessness.

Despite his claims of the heart's central role in cognition,
Aristotle attributed mental illness to brain dysfunction.
If the brain cannot absorb heat from the heart, the heart

will react quickly and recklessly to any disturbance. Just think about the feeling of anger. Your heart beats faster and you feel a bit hotter. In Aristotle's anatomical dissections, the brain was naturally cold and in a good position to balance the heat. While we metaphorically advise the aggressors in our lives to *cool their tempers*, this advice is grounded in an ancient understanding of physiology.

Without realizing it, Aristotle had been describing the sympathetic nervous system. In response to stressful situations—let's say, an unpleasant encounter with a Grizzly bear—the brain prepares the body for fight or flight. Among many other biological changes, the preparation consists of improving blood circulation by raising the heart rate. However, this rise in heart rate is a consequence of the stress response, not responsible for it. Really, it is the nervous system, an extension of the brain, that governs heart rate, not the other way around.

While science has moved on, Aristotle's thoughts on the connection between our bodies and our senses still breathes in our language. We still think of the heart as the seat of emotion and the brain as the center of cool, logical thinking. Perhaps this is a further testament to Aristotle's impressive legacy. His influence has been cast so far that even his wrong ideas have left a footprint on us (adapted from Mandal, 2016).

* * *

We may still have something to learn from Aristotle's concept of a bodily basis for mental health. In his account, mental illnesses like depression arise from an imbalance between the brain and the rest of the body, with depression characterized by an overly *cool* physiology. Like some of his contemporaries, Aristotle adopted the concept of four humors—blood, yellow bile, black bile, and phlegm—that regulate human behavior.

In this framework, depression or, as he called it, *melancholia*, was believed to result from an excess of black bile. Other premodern thinkers believed that depression reflected not a physical disease but rather a spiritual one. They posited that demonic possession caused depression, and only punitive methods like exorcism, burning, beating, or solitary confinement could cure it.

The fact that modern medicine divides into specialties with names stemming from these ideologies speaks to how the history of mental health continues to impact our current practice. For instance, we still differentiate between the field of psychiatry ("healing of the soul" in Greek) and the field of neurology ("the study of nerves"), though recent research has continually proven how interconnected they are. Why is medicine still practiced this way? Professor Ed Bullmore, a psychiatrist from the University of Cambridge, blames René Descartes.

In his book *The Inflamed Mind*, Dr. Bullmore describes a patient he calls *Mrs. P*, whom he met while training as a physician before he specialized in psychiatry. Mrs. P had rheumatoid arthritis, an inflammatory disease affecting the joints, causing painful swelling in the hands and knees. After talking through Mrs. P's symptoms, all of which were indicative of rheumatoid arthritis, Dr. Bullmore asked her some additional questions: "Could you tell me about your state of mind? How is your mood?"

Over the next ten minutes, Mrs. P explained she had very little energy, was commonly occupied by guilty and pessimistic thoughts, had poor sleep, and nothing gave her pleasure anymore. Mrs. P had all of the telltale signs of depression.

Proud of his clinical discovery, Dr. Bullmore reported to his superior that Mrs. P presents not just with rheumatoid arthritis but also depression. The senior physician was not impressed.

"Depressed? Well, you would be, wouldn't you?"

The standard medical thinking goes as follows: Mrs. P is depressed because she lives with a chronic inflammatory disease she knows will not get better. Depression was her state of mind and did not relate to her physical symptoms. In fact, it would be impossible to diagnose Mrs. P with depression since the official guidelines explicitly exclude this diagnosis if the symptoms can be attributed to the effects of another medical condition.

Mrs. P's story is not unique. About 90 percent of patients with rheumatoid arthritis list fatigue as their primary complaint and about 40 percent of these patients bear the symptoms of depression (National Rheumatoid Arthritis Society, 2014). There is also some anecdotal evidence that treating the inflammation can relieve the depressive symptoms. Referred to as a *Remicade high*, nurses at the University College London have reported that arthritis patients treated with an anti-inflammatory medication immediately experienced a better mood and profound gratitude. These pleasant reactions could simply result from receiving an effective treatment for their physical disease. But the fact that many physicians have been slow to consider a direct link between depressive symptoms and bodily illness stems from a deeper schism: the philosophy of mind-body dualism established by Descartes.

In contrast to Aristotle's embodied concept of cognition, Descartes thought of the mind and body as completely separate entities. According to Descartes, each person is composed of both a physical body that interacts with the surrounding world and a nonphysical mind responsible for thought and self-awareness. There is an intuitive appeal to the notion of mind-body dualism. It can be difficult to believe that the abstract processes underlying consciousness and decision-making have their basis in physical substances like organic compounds and chemicals.

Yet dualism suffers from a litany of problems to which Descartes was not naive. For instance, even if mind and body are separate, it is clear the two must interact, such that decisions made by the mind can cause bodily movements, and that bodily sensations can affect mental processes. But how could a physical entity and a nonphysical entity possibly interact?

Descartes proposed a bridge between mind and body via the pineal gland, a pea-shaped structure bathed in a pool of fluid located in the center of the brain. Yet subsequent research showed that this structure is not nearly as consequential as Descartes claimed. And even his contemporaries pointed out that his explanation simply dodges the question and poses another one: how does a nonphysical mind interact with a physical pineal gland? However, these problems did not stop Cartesian dualism from entering medical discourse and framing medicine's approach to psychiatric disorders.

The lingering legacy of dualism still affects how patients receive care. Most of the physicians that Mrs. P would likely encounter have little training for treating her problems holistically. Just as the hammer sees every problem as a nail, a rheumatologist would be unlikely to ask her any questions about depression or think about addressing such issues as a part of her care. In turn, a psychiatrist Mrs. P might see for her depressed mood may not consider her inflammatory disease as relevant to her psychiatric symptoms. Since doctors and scientists tend to specialize in a narrow range of topics, many interdisciplinary questions of clinical import have been historically under-addressed. This is starting to change, and a prime example is the budding field of neuroimmunology.

* * *

Scientists have traditionally thought that the brain is effectively separated from the rest of the body by the blood-brain barrier, a molecular mascot of Cartesian dualism. The blood-brain barrier refers to a collection of structures that prevents most chemicals and cells from entering the brain through the bloodstream. Because the blood-brain barrier was thought to keep immune cells and chemicals out of the brain, doctors have historically dismissed the idea that inflammatory conditions like rheumatoid arthritis could affect brain function. However, it is now clear that some chemicals of the immune system can jump the fence and activate microglia, the brain's resident immune cells. These activated microglia can then attack brain structures that coordinate emotional responses, such as the amygdala.

Altogether, the recent findings in neuroimmunology provide a plausible story that links inflammation to mental disturbances like depression. Since doctors can track biomarkers of inflammation by measuring the levels of specific chemicals in the blood, this research offers an opportunity to monitor a possible cause of depression.

If inflammation can cause depression, then what causes inflammation? In addition to infection and injury, stress can also trigger inflammation. Remember the Grizzly bear from earlier, who served as our example of a stressor that can trigger a fight or flight response? Acute stressful events like running into a bear will activate the immune system, but these effects are temporary and should go away once the situation is over. However, if the stressor never really stops, then neither does the inflammation. If the bear comes to your home every night, then the inflammatory nightmare never ends.

Scientists believe that the inflammation triggered by chronic stress may be one of the mechanisms by which adverse childhood experiences (commonly abbreviated as ACEs) increase the risk of depression. In a landmark 1998 study, Dr. Vincent Filetti and colleagues asked a straightforward question: how do early life events influence health in adulthood? They started by introducing a concept that would later be called an ACE score.

The ACE score quantifies the number of adverse events a person experienced before their eighteenth birthday (Center on the Developing Child at Harvard University, 2019). Calculating your ACE score involves answering a series of difficult questions, like "Did a parent or other adult in the household ever throw something at you?" or "Did you live with anyone who went to prison?" A point is added each time you answer "yes." Using a test like this, Filetti and colleagues discovered a tight relationship between ACEs and a wide range of poor health outcomes, including a 4.5-fold increased risk of depression among adults who scored 4 or higher.

Consistent with what we know about stress and inflammation, it has been shown that people with high ACE scores tend to also have increased levels of inflammatory biomarkers (Lacey et al., 2020). Individuals with depression also tend to have high inflammation (Lee and Giuliani, 2019). However, the evidence indicates that inflammation is not the only reason why adverse childhood experiences are so strongly related to depression (Iob and Steptoe, 2019). Child psychologists have identified several different reasons why a tough childhood can lead individuals to be depressed later in life, including psychological trauma and reduced social support (Cheong et al., 2017). Inflammation may just be one of many causes, but it is still an important one since it can be monitored before symptoms arise and be directly treated.

What are the implications of this avenue of research for proactive approaches to brain diseases? Currently, there is no blood test or brain scan that can tell you if you have depression. Psychiatrists evaluate patients based on their subjective experience across time to determine the presence of a mental health disorder. For major depressive disorder in adults, diagnostic criteria are met if a patient experiences regular episodes of five out of the following nine symptoms: depressed mood, loss of interest/pleasure, weight loss or gain, abnormal sleep, psychomotor agitation or slowness, fatigue, inappropriate guilt, decreased concentration, and thoughts of death or suicide.

In our current system, diagnoses can only be made on the basis of experienced symptoms. As such, diagnoses are often made after a patient has already experienced challenges with daily functioning. At this point, patients have had time to try to cope with their symptoms on their own, sometimes through drugs and alcohol or isolating from friends and family. Mental health resources could help these individuals but seeking needed support can be both a stigmatizing and cumbersome experience. It is a damning truth that it is far easier to visit the liquor store than to schedule an appointment with a psychiatrist.

These issues are not unique to psychiatry and finding better biomarkers for mental illness will not solve everything. Nevertheless, few can deny the clinical and preventive potential of being able to catch early signs of depression by screening blood samples, just as doctors diagnose diabetes.

Finally, we must also consider how we can intervene against depression even earlier, given what we know about the adverse childhood experiences often at the root of it all. ACE scoring is a powerful tool that gives the health provider a window into a wide range of conditions a person is at risk of acquiring because of their upbringing. A provider can use this information to direct mental health resources to the children and young adults who need them most. Some states, like California, have implemented ACE screening to help providers identify individuals who may benefit from early interventions, such as family education on toxic stress or referral to behavioral health specialists (Let's Get Healthy California, 2022).

"Imagine if there were such a thing as a 'Coughing Disorder'," asks Richard Dear, a PhD student with Dr. Bullmore, during a 2021 interview with Gates Cambridge. "Doctors can see you are coughing but have no idea if the cough is caused by Covid, tuberculosis, or something stuck in your throat. These underlying causes all need different treatments but imagine doctors don't even agree on the range of possibilities. That is where we are with depression today."

The first step in developing better proactive measures to treat depression will be to identify all of its possible causes, as well as better methods to screen for those underlying causes in individual patients. ACE screening reflects one already-available tool that can identify individuals at risk of both mental and physical health disorders. The current research suggests that blood-based markers of inflammation could be another way of monitoring a potential cause of depression, similar to how a PCR (polymerase chain reaction) test can identify SARS-CoV2 as the agent responsible for a patient's "Coughing Disorder."

What does the current research say about treating depression with anti-inflammatory medications? A recent meta-analysis summarizing the results of thirty randomized controlled trials showed that anti-inflammatory medications could reduce depressive symptoms (Bai et al., 2020). While this is a good start, the anti-depressant effects from each study were small, and the clinical benefit for any individual patient may be limited.

To optimize these anti-depressant effects, psychiatrists will need to figure out which anti-inflammatory agents to use, at what doses, and in which individuals. It may be that only a subset of patients with depression who have high inflammation will significantly benefit from anti-inflammatory medications. Given that all current treatments for depression are reactive to symptoms, a proactive therapy targeted against a biomarker would be a momentous advance for the field of psychiatry.

This story speaks to the importance of looking beyond the brain for solutions to neuropsychiatric problems. Every day, neuroscientists are learning more about how an untamed immune system can cause all types of mental disturbances, including hallucinations, memory loss, and depressed mood. As Aristotle understood, albeit imperfectly, mental function requires a balance among the whole body as a system, not simply the mind or brain in isolation.

CHAPTER 5

SOMETIMES IT HITS YOU IN THE HEAD WITH A BAT

In neuroscience courses, it is common to encounter the story of Jean-Dominique Bauby, a former editor in chief of *Elle* magazine, who suffered a stroke to the brainstem. Housed in the brainstem live white matter tracts that allow the brain to communicate with the rest of the body, so injuries here can cause paralysis of all or nearly all muscles. This is what happened to Bauby, as his stroke led to a condition called *locked-in syndrome* where he lost the ability to move any muscle in his body except for his left eyelid.

Using just one eyelid, he maintained communication with the outside world by blinking once to signal *yes*, or twice for *no*. Bauby also managed to form sentences in his own way. Visitors would read a frequency-ordered alphabet of the French language to Bauby (E, S, A, R, ...), and once uttering his intended letter, he would blink. He even wrote a whole book this way. *The Diving Bell and the Butterfly* contains imaginative stories of adventures to distant lands and reflections on his serious condition, all in testament of his preserved cerebral cortex, which spared his higher cognitive functions.

Rebecca is another creative with a story of disability and perseverance. Like Bauby, Rebecca relied on a tool for communication. Hers was more efficient: an eye-tracking device called *Tobii Dynavox* allowed her to type words with her pupils. While Tobii can translate eye movements to spoken words in any desired voice, Rebecca chose to convey her words in a fancy British accent. American-born Rebecca loved the irony behind her new voice, a surrogate speaker that became necessary because of her deteriorating condition.

Rebecca had ALS (amyotrophic lateral sclerosis), a disease of widespread fame due to its association with legendary baseball player Lou Gehrig, as well as the viral sensation of 2014: The Ice Bucket Challenge. Despite the massive popularity of the Ice Bucket Challenge, the tribulations of ALS are not always appreciated. It involves the degeneration of the neurons that control movement, beginning innocuously with muscle weakness in the hands and feet. Rebecca's first symptom was *foot drop*, an inability to lift the front of the foot as it drags along the floor during walking.

These symptoms quickly worsen. Limb movement is affected, and issues with speech and swallowing arise. ALS becomes fatal once the disease assumes control over the muscles that orchestrate breathing, which tends to happen between two to four years after diagnosis.

When patients face terminal diagnoses, there can be an urge to crystallize their legacy. Some manifest a piece of art, a last word before passing. The neurosurgeon Paul Kalanithi spent his final days writing his memoir, *When Breath Becomes Air,* before dying from lung cancer. Jean-Dominique Bauby's death came two days after the publication of *The Diving Bell and The Butterfly.* Rebecca yearned to create with the time she had left, even as ALS stole her voice.

A film director with twenty-five years of experience, Rebecca needed to get behind the camera. Wheelchair-bound and strapped up with cowboy boots, she shouted commands like "cut!" and "action!" from her British-voiced Tobii for ALS public service announcements.

She aspired to direct a full-length movie. A script about the sole survivor of a house fire, who draws scrutiny for acting with nonchalance following the traumatic event, caught her eye. To her, it was a story about how people grieve in unpredictable ways. Some of her friends questioned her commitment to continue working after her fatal diagnosis. Her reply was direct: "Why should I stop doing what I love?"

Unfortunately, there would be no Hollywood ending for Rebecca's final movie. Her eye movements started to fail, and Tobii could no longer pick up on them. She spent her last months exactly how she wanted, surrounded by her husband and their two kids. They renewed vows, took a final vacation, even survived a pandemic together. Two and a half years after her diagnosis, Rebecca died peacefully at home, surrounded by family.

* * *

When confronted with a devastating reality such as a terminal illness, it is natural to wonder what caused the tragedy. Is it something we can make sense of, or even prevent? For around 90 percent of patients with ALS, the cause is totally unclear—these are sporadic cases with no family history of the disease. But Rebecca did have a family history of neurological conditions. Her mother had dementia, and her grandfather also had ALS. Genetic testing revealed that Rebecca was among the 10 percent of patients who inherit a genetic mutation known to cause ALS in some and frontotemporal dementia in others. While tragic for the affected families, patients with genetic forms of ALS can provide important clues regarding the cause of the condition, thus informing the development of new therapies aimed at reversing the disease.

To understand the new treatments in the field of medical genetics, it helps to become familiar with a set of principles that biologists call the *central dogma*. All of the instructions to make and run a body are contained within DNA (deoxyribonucleic acid), genetic material that is inherited from one's biological mother and father. Contained within DNA are genes, sequences of base pairs that represent the ingredients to create molecules that are essential for life. The instructions from genes are transcribed into a molecular middleman called messenger RNA (ribonucleic acid), which is then translated to make protein. DNA mutations cause genetic diseases, resulting in mutant proteins that either fail to perform a critical life process or become toxic to the body.

The central dogma highlights two truths that are crucial for our story. Because DNA is inherited from one's parents, a genetic disease can pass from generation to generation. Inheriting just one copy of the gene in Rebecca's family from one's mother or father is enough to guarantee a future of neurological disease. However, the central dogma also suggests a possible treatment for genetic diseases. While it's difficult to erase something written in your DNA, what if you could shoot the messenger, silencing the RNA destined to make a problematic protein?

Some genes have fun, catchy names, like Sonic Hedgehog, a crucial coordinator of body development. Or Diablo, a ruthless decider of life or death for the cell. The mutated gene for Rebecca has a less playful name: *C9orf72*. It also has a fairly complicated and imperfectly understood function.

C9orf72 appears to be involved in the transport of cellular packages within neurons. Like a bustling city, a cell needs an infrastructure to deliver the right materials to the right locations. A mutation in *C9orf72* will impair that infrastructure, leading to a buildup of toxic elements in neurons. Deficiencies in cellular trafficking are believed to be one reason why *C9orf72* mutations can cause ALS (or dementia, as observed in Rebecca's mother). However, it is not the full story.

There is a segment of the normal *C9orf72* gene sequence that seems redundant—a repeat of the same six base pairs (GGGGCC) between twenty and thirty times. Repeating sequences in genes are fairly common and not cause for concern. In health, these repeats are intronic, which means they do not code for any part of the protein. In the disease-causing *C9orf72* gene, however, there are hundreds of GGGGCC repeats. When these many repeats are stringed together, two problems arise. First, the normal function of the protein is compromised, causing defects in cell trafficking. Second, the GGG-GCC sequences become coded into small proteins that are toxic to neurons.

When the field of medical genetics was young, the common thought was that treating diseases caused by a single mutation would be relatively straightforward. You would simply need to fix the mutated gene using the advanced gene-editing tools of the day, and that would cure the patient. However, twenty years after the completion of the Human Genome Project, most monogenic diseases remain incurable, including sickle cell disease, cystic fibrosis, and Huntington's disease. Why is this the case, when sophisticated gene-editing technologies are in the news each day?

While gene-editing tools are great at modifying genes in a dish, it is currently not possible to use them to edit each cell within an affected organ. Instead, what is possible is to interfere with the expression of a problematic gene using an antisense oligonucleotide (ASO).

An ASO is a small, modifiable molecule that can silence any gene it is designed to target by blocking its messenger RNA. For example, a simple ASO against *C9orf72* would limit the amount of its protein in the body, reducing the levels of toxic buildup in a cell. However, a simple strategy like this cannot work against *C9orf72*, or many other disease-causing mutations. Too much mutant *C9orf72* is a problem, but so is not having enough regular *C9orf72*, which is needed for cellular trafficking.

Dr. Robert Brown's lab at the University of Massachusetts is working on a solution to this conundrum (Tran et al., 2021). His group has leveraged the fact that three different types of messenger RNA copies of the *C9orf72* gene are made in the cell: two of which contain the repeat expansion and a third that does not. Their ASO selectively eliminates the two types of gene copies that produce the toxic byproduct. As a result, the patient's neurons should have enough healthy *C9orf72* to perform normal cellular functions while reducing the disease-causing toxins. So far, one patient with ALS has received these special ASOs. The patient's toxins did reduce substantially, and their symptoms have remained stable. This experimental treatment is currently in clinical trials to confirm its safety and evaluate its clinical efficacy.

* * *

Promising results like these mean a lot for Rebecca's son, Cody, who is currently an MD/PhD student training to become both a physician and a scientist. Cody bears the same *C9orf72* mutation as his mother. Without an improvement in our current treatments, he will likely share a similar fate, acquiring ALS or dementia at too young an age.

Cody was dedicated to neuroscience research before his mother's diagnosis, working in a memory lab on the same hospital floor where she received care. But like many things in his life, his research interests changed after learning of his mother's illness.

"Sometimes you're looking at the forest floor for a subtle sign of where to go, and sometimes it hits you in the head with a bat," Cody said to me in an interview. Bearing this intense personal connection to ALS woven into his own DNA, it was clear that he had a calling to do whatever he could to stop this illness in its tracks.

Cody is in an incredibly rare position where he can contribute to the battle against ALS from all angles—as an advocate, a patient, a researcher, and eventually, as a physician. With the same twenty-four hours each of us mortals are granted each day, he finds the time to capitalize on all of these different roles.

Cody helps fundraise for ALS research, collaborating with his partner to develop "Fuck ALS" T-shirts, along with other merchandise. He enrolls himself in clinical trials as a presymptomatic patient, allowing scientists to collect his data and learn more about how the *C9orf72* mutation affects an individual before they become sick. He has donated his own cells to science, which have been transformed into motor neurons that bear the *C9orf72* mutation. Finally, Cody is a scientist, working with cells from other ALS patients like him to better understand the role of cellular trafficking in the disease.

Undergoing genetic testing to determine your risk for conditions like ALS is scary, especially when no cures currently exist. If you had a predisposition to acquire Alzheimer's disease at the age of fifty, would you want to know when you turn eighteen or remain in ignorant bliss?

"There's certainly a lot of costs to knowing," Cody said when reflecting on his own decision to get genetic testing. "If I were to talk to somebody considering making this decision, I would emphasize those costs. You do wake up in the middle of the night and your foot feels weird, like everyone's does, and now you got a ground truth that is very terrifying."

Cody ultimately decided to undergo testing because knowledge is power. He wanted his long-term partner to know about his potential for future health needs. He wanted to be able to enroll in clinical studies if he was positive for the mutation and aid in the fight for a cure.

Most people, if informed of the possibility that their lifespan could be shortened by an insidious medical condition, would not opt for a rigorous eight-year training program culminating in two doctoral degrees. But Cody made the difficult decision to pursue an MD and a PhD because of his faith in clinical neuroscience research.

"It's something that can be fixed," Cody states carefully, balancing the skepticism of a scientist with the hope of a future patient. "I made the decision to spend eight years of my life in school, despite on paper right now having a significantly shortened lifespan, because I believe that things will work out for me."

From the Ice Bucket Challenge to the custom-made T-shirts dropping the F-bomb on a neuromuscular disorder, ALS has captivated the world's attention because of its effects on young lives. From the money raised by such efforts, we have learned about the genes that can cause ALS and how one may block the pernicious molecular cascades triggered by those genes. This genetic approach to therapeutic development applies not just to ALS but to all sorts of brain diseases that tend to run in families, including Alzheimer's disease, epilepsy, schizophrenia, and others.

Genetics plays a two-fold role in our fight against brain disease. It helps us better understand a medical condition's root causes and identify patients who may benefit from personalized therapies early before their symptoms arise. The fact that pathology can be written into the body's code at birth highlights an uncomfortable reality applicable to several brain disorders: early events and exposures can trigger future disease. What can we do to prevent these disease-causing triggers?

CHAPTER 6

WHEN SELF ATTACKS BRAIN

Not commonly will you see tears shed on the carpets at the annual Vanity Fair Oscar Party. But 2019 was a special year. Selma Blair, an actress famous for her roles in movies like *Legally Blonde* and *Cruel Intentions*, had brought a cane to the red carpet. It was her first public appearance since being diagnosed with multiple sclerosis (MS) six months earlier.

"When I heard on Instagram...so many people [saying] 'you've done so much for me and now I can go out and use this and not be ashamed,' and I'm like 'wait, wait, hold on, don't get a hideous one!'" She would later say in the 2021 documentary *Introducing, Selma Blair*. Maintaining her good humor, she urges her fans with disabilities to purchase stylish canes that you can still buy on a budget.

Blair's cane was custom-made, designed to meet the occasion. Complete with a pink diamond and an inscription with her monogram, her walking tool matched her block-patterned, floor-length dress (Stump, 2019). While some may mistake this exuberance for vanity, her personalized cane conveyed a powerful message to the wider community: disability does not have to come at the cost of fashion or any other personal indulgence that brings one joy.

Many of the most prevalent neurological diseases, such as Parkinson's or Alzheimer's disease, only start to bear their effect in old age. Multiple sclerosis is different in that it predominantly affects young adults. Most patients that receive a diagnosis are in their late twenties. MS is an autoimmune disease resulting from the body's own immune system attacking the brain.

In Chapter four, we discussed how bodily inflammation could affect brain function, leading to the symptoms of depression. The type of immune activity involved in multiple sclerosis is a little different. While inflammation in response to acute stress is nonspecific, attacking anything in its vicinity, multiple sclerosis is primarily a disease of the stealthy assassins of the body: the lymphocytes.

The mission of the lymphocyte is to target a specific nemesis, such as the SARS-CoV2 virus that causes COVID-19. The lymphocytes need to react just to molecules foreign to the body but not to molecules within the body to perform their job well. How do the lymphocytes know which molecules are foreign and which molecules belong to self?

During their development, lymphocytes encounter self-molecules via the bloodstream. The cells that react to self are sent for destruction, leaving behind only the lymphocytes that can attack foreign agents. But there is a hole in this clever trick. Some self-molecules do not enter the bloodstream, such as those in the brain, which is insulated from the rest of the body by the blood-brain barrier.

Multiple sclerosis occurs when lymphocytes find a way to leak through the blood-brain barrier and attack specific structures in the brain. In MS, the body's immune cells attack myelin, a fatty substance found predominantly in white matter. As discussed in Chapters one and two, white matter composes the highways of the brain, crucial for communication between distant brain regions.

No two patients with multiple sclerosis are alike because the disease affects different regions of white matter in different people, resulting in different neurological problems. I once met a patient with MS who noted eye pain and blurry vision before an MRI scan of her optic nerve revealed a shiny brightness that wasn't supposed to be there.

Selma Blair's first symptoms were pain and fatigue. She found herself needing to pull over on the side of the road to sleep after dropping her son off at school, unable to go fifteen minutes without a nap (*Good Morning America*, 2019). Because the first symptoms a patient may notice are not unique to MS, making a correct diagnosis early in the course of the disease can be difficult. Selma's doctors dismissed her initial symptoms as the normal consequences of a stressful life.

Multiple sclerosis presents in episodes marked by the worsening of symptoms, intermitted by times of peace, characterized by no new symptom onset. The cyclic nature of symptom severity follows the patterns of immune infiltration into the brain and the brain's ability to recover from these self-inflicted wounds.

Lymphocytes will leak through the blood-brain barrier, destroy myelin, and call in other immune cells to join in the attack. When this happens, plaques form in the brain, causing the symptoms to get worse for the patient. Eventually, regulatory immune cells will arrive at the scene, temporarily arresting further carnage. In this time of peace, the brain can recover as immature brain cells replenish the missing myelin. But this ability to remyelinate is lost over time, leading to less and less recovery as more episodes ensue.

It took an especially bad episode for Selma to finally receive a diagnosis. She had been dropping things and falling to the ground. Her leg would keep bouncing, and her pinky would not stop moving. Selma even reached out to Michael J. Fox before her diagnosis, thinking she might have Parkinson's disease like him. Finally, a fall she suffered in front of a doctor earned her an MRI scan.

Dalmatian spots covered her brain scan, engraved with bright areas that reflected new insults and black holes corresponding to dead tissue. Her diagnosis of multiple sclerosis solidified, Selma sighed with relief. "No one ever believed me," Selma explained in a 2022 interview on

The View, until a brain scan proved her problems had an organic source.

Most patients are understandably reluctant to be seen in public during an episode of MS. Yet Selma understands that her status as a celebrity can grant this disease visibility that will trigger more public awareness. Such visibility is crucial for under-diagnosed conditions like multiple sclerosis, which could be identified earlier and attract more research funding if more people were aware of the disease.

Selma has taken steps to show the public what living with multiple sclerosis is like. She walked the red carpet with a cane. She speaks candidly about her condition to reporters. She even gives interviews on *Good Morning America* during episodes of multiple sclerosis, when her speech screeches and stutters as she fights through sentences.

In her 2019 *Good Morning America* interview, Selma reflected on the courage and confidence required to speak to the public in such a state. "I was a little scared of talking, but even my neurologist said, 'no, this will bring a lot of awareness because no one has the energy to talk when they're in a flare-up.' But I do because I love a camera!"

By combining her mission to spread awareness with her comfort around cameras, Selma has now produced a documentary titled *Introducing, Selma Blair*, inviting viewers into her world as an MS patient. Selma's documentary also introduces the public to a new, experimental treatment for multiple sclerosis that holds promise for patients with especially aggressive forms of the disease: hematopoietic stem cell transplantation.

* * *

Researchers originally developed hematopoietic stem cell transplantation (HSCT) as a treatment for patients with blood cancers like multiple myeloma or leukemia. The idea behind HSCT is to reboot the immune system to treat diseases where the patient's immune cells are causing the problem (Craven, 2019). All of a person's blood cells, including red blood cells, which deliver oxygen, and white blood cells that make up the immune system, originate from a common ancestor called a hematopoietic stem cell.

If we eliminated all of a patient's white blood cells, the hematopoietic stem cell population could replenish the body with its requisite immune cells in a matter of months. This is an attractive feature for patients with leukemia because they harbor cancerous white blood cells, which need to be eliminated and replaced with healthy immune cells to treat the disease. Hematopoietic stem cells also bear therapeutic potential for patients with multiple sclerosis since white blood cells are also implicated in their disease.

While the acronym HSCT contains the word *transplantation*, the procedure does not usually involve a transplant between two individuals. Transplanting blood cells from one individual to another can be problematic since the donor's immune cells can attack the recipient in a complication known as *graft-versus-host disease*. Instead, HSCT typically involves the following.

First, a physician will extract and store the patient's own hematopoietic stem cells. Then, chemotherapy will be administered, eliminating virtually all white blood cells, including both the healthy and diseased cells. Following chemotherapy, the hematopoietic stem cells are returned to the patient to help the body rebuild the immune system anew. While the immune system is recovering, the patient is kept in a sterile environment and closely monitored for any infections, which would need immediate treatment if found since the body's defenses are down. After a few weeks of close monitoring in the hospital, the patient can return home and can expect their immune system to recover within three to twelve months.

Selma's doctors are honest with her about the prospects of HSCT for her condition. It will not undo already caused brain damage. Rather, the intent is to prevent the disease from getting worse by eliminating the immune cells that cross through her blood-brain barrier, attacking the myelin in her brain. In terms of stopping the progression of the disease, HSCT is quite effective, comparing favorably to other multiple sclerosis treatments. Around 80 percent of MS patients who receive HSCT exhibit no evidence of further disease after two years (Murraro et al., 2017). However, the chemotherapy regimen is grueling, and there is a risk of death with HSCT, which means doctors and patients should pursue this only in aggressive, treatment-resistant cases.

Did the treatment work? It is impossible to say at first. HSCT does not reverse the disease, and so Selma's usual problems with speech and movement persist. Yet she has been able to return to activities that would otherwise be exceedingly difficult, like horseback riding and swimming in the pool. It has been over two years since her procedure in 2019, and she has remained in remission from multiple sclerosis—no new lesions have formed.

When asked on *Good Morning America* in 2021 how the treatment affected her, Selma reflected on the transformative nature of such a difficult medical journey: "I am a different person. I chose this as a marker in my life to want to live, to want to be a person who can show other people with a chronic illness that resilience is possible." Her story is one that fundamentally revolves around the human desire to flourish, even in times of hardship. The best thing that a doctor can do is provide for patients that right.

* * *

But what if medicine could prevent multiple sclerosis altogether? Even with the most advanced treatments available, never was there talk about reversing Selma's condition, undoing the brain damage caused by decades of inflammation. Medicine cannot provide a time machine, but it can change the future for individuals at risk of acquiring her disease.

To prevent people from ever getting MS, we need a good understanding of what causes the disease in the first place. A recent study has shed light on the roots of multiple sclerosis, consequently suggesting a strategy that could protect the whole world from this condition.

When I was in fifth grade, the most interesting set of objects to me were the twenty-six volumes of the encyclopedia that sat in my elementary school homeroom, each book corresponding to every letter of the English alphabet. I would scour these encyclopedias for fancy words I could not pronounce, aiming to impress my parents with sophisticated vocabulary.

One day, I asked my dad about a word I had found in the volume for the letter M: mononucleosis. Despite struggling with the second half of the word, he knew what I meant. A primary care physician, my father explained that mononucleosis is an infectious disease characterized by a sore throat and a fever, and there is no vaccine against the virus that causes it.

About five years later, I would learn two more things about mononucleosis after a high school friend contracted it. First, it turns out that adults also have trouble with the condition's tricky name and simply call it *mono*. Second, I learned why vaccine development against its causative agent, Epstein-Barr Virus, was not a major priority. Outside of the embarrassment of contracting mono, also known as the *kissing disease*, it is relatively benign and goes away on its own.

Scientists are now learning that Epstein-Barr Virus (EBV) is not as innocuous as it once seemed. The virus infects lymphocytes, the same category of cells tasked with defending the body against foreign agents. While most of the time, the infection self-resolves, EBV can cause lymphocytes to proliferate, resulting in a cancer called lymphoma.

But the potential long-term sequelae of an EBV infection don't stop there. A 2022 study of over ten million military veterans showed that Epstein-Barr Virus is likely the causative agent behind almost all cases of multiple sclerosis.

"Left, face! Right, face!" Doug tries his best to keep up with the commands without making it obvious that he is a rookie. Keeping his back straight and his movements smooth, he snaps to his left and to his right at the orders of the drill sergeant, a challenge after many years on the couch. Doug joined the military for the same reason many young men do—to escape troubles at home and gain the opportunity to travel. A foster child since the age of five, he had never seen the world outside of his home state of Maryland. The military offered a refuge of discipline and adventure.

Before joining the military, Doug received no routine medical care. Outside of an encounter with the emergency room after falling out of a tree, he rarely visited the hospital or doctor's office. This all changed after he enlisted. Cadets are routinely tested for a palate of infectious agents to ensure that no virus compromises the national defense of the United States of America.

Doug never acquired multiple sclerosis. He ended up attending an Ivy League university after his stint in the military, and then he became a colleague of mine later in his academic career. But if one of his friends in the military did develop MS, physicians would be able to trace all of the viruses that this person was exposed to before their diagnosis since they are screened for viral infections so regularly.

Over a twenty-year period, Dr. Kjetil Bjorvenik and colleagues identified 801 veterans with multiple sclerosis. They found evidence of a prior Epstein-Barr Virus infection in all but one of these cases. Comparing the military veterans with MS to demographically similar veterans without MS, they found that a prior EBV infection was associated with a thirty-two-fold increased risk of acquiring multiple sclerosis. To put that number in perspective, cigarette smoking results in about a fifteen- to thirty-fold increased risk of lung cancer (Centers for Disease Control and Prevention, 2021). Since virtually every subject with MS had evidence of a prior EBV infection, the researchers concluded that Epstein-Barr Virus exposure is likely necessary for developing multiple sclerosis.

What makes Epstein-Barr Virus such a huge risk factor for acquiring MS? Scientists aren't sure, but a leading theory is the molecular mimicry hypothesis. When a virus attacks the body, the immune system responds by recruiting lymphocytes to vanquish the enemy. In addition to defeating the virus, the lymphocytes also help the immune system adapt so that this pathogen will never be a problem ever again.

Some lymphocytes produce molecules called antibodies which will bind to the virus if it ever returns, signaling it for destruction. However, the Epstein-Barr Virus is composed of proteins that look very similar to myelin, the fatty substance attacked in MS. According to the molecular mimicry idea, antibodies against EBV may cross the blood-brain barrier and bind to healthy myelin, signaling lymphocytes and other immune cells to infiltrate and attack (Lanz et al., 2022).

Note that while Epstein-Barr Virus infection is common, multiple sclerosis is significantly rarer. Ninety-five percent of adults become infected with EBV at some point in their life, so it is clear the infection is harmless in most people. Many other factors are involved in determining which EBV-infected individuals eventually acquire MS, including genetics, environment, and nutrition. Nevertheless, the relationship between Epstein-Barr Virus and MS is important since it implies that if we can prevent the former, we can also prevent the latter.

Some of the same players who developed vaccines against COVID-19 are beginning human trials to test the safety and efficacy of an Epstein-Barr Virus vaccine. The biotechnology company Moderna has developed a new vaccine against EBV, which is currently undergoing Phase 1 trials as of January 2022. The original intention of Moderna's product was to prevent cases of mononucleosis, but news of the link between Epstein-Barr Virus and multiple sclerosis has caused a surge of interest in an effective vaccine.

Imagine if, in a few years, you could go to your primary care physician's office and get a preventive vaccine for multiple sclerosis. Just like you can for COVID-19, or annually for the flu, just like millions of women do to prevent cervical cancer from ever occurring. A vaccine against Epstein-Barr Virus could deliver this promise, relegating MS to the sidelines.

If someone had written this book seventy years ago, there probably would have been a chapter dedicated to poliomyelitis, or polio, a paralyzing disease caused by the poliovirus. Through widespread vaccination against poliovirus, public health initiatives have largely eradicated poliomyelitis from most global communities, in stark contrast to the polio epidemics of the 1950s. Perhaps seventy years from now, this chapter on multiple sclerosis will read like an ancient relic, an ode to a disease that no longer exists.

CHAPTER 7

CAN ALZHEIMER'S DISEASE BE PREVENTED?

"Stamp, leg... tent, motor... menu. That's all I got!"

Sister Mary is putting on a performance that proves that she is special for her age. The Catholic nun, who recently celebrated her one hundred and first birthday, is being assessed for her memory capacity through a Delayed Recall test, wherein she must repeat as many items as possible from a ten-word list shown to her five minutes ago. This assessment completed, she moves on to the Verbal Fluency Test, where she lists as many animals she can think of in sixty seconds:

"Cat, dog, bird, rat, squirrel, chicken... pig... monkey."

Sister Mary brings her A-game to clinical assessments. She has developed a strategy to quickly rattle off all the words that come to mind as soon as possible, leaving her time to mine the deeply buried words from within her brain. Her memory has been tested every day for decades as if she had prepared for this moment her entire life.

Although she received only eight years of formal education in her youth, Sister Mary taught at a parochial middle school for sixty-five years, spending the summers taking courses to make up for the classes she missed after eighth grade (Snowdon, 1999). Even after "retiring" from the schoolroom at eighty-four, she never stopped stimulating the minds of others. The eighty-five-pound, four-foot-five-inch nun would continue to deliver lessons to her Sisters in the convent while also staying informed of the latest news and literature with the aid of her trusty magnifying glass. Eager to contribute to human knowledge at every stage of her life, she jumped at the opportunity to donate her time and, eventually, her brain to the study of Alzheimer's disease.

People often use the terms Alzheimer's disease and dementia interchangeably, but they're not exactly the same thing. Alzheimer's disease is a neurodegenerative disorder that can be strongly suspected while one is still living, but the diagnosis is only solidified at autopsy when its characteristic features are witnessed in the brain. Alzheimer's disease is the most common cause of dementia, a term that refers to a state of worsening cognitive impairment related to aging. Alzheimer's disease causes a specific type of dementia, characterized by memory problems, as opposed to other types of dementias initiated by other pathologies, which may primarily affect personality or language ability.

Although doctors cannot prove the diagnosis until autopsy, primary care physicians can identify individuals who likely have Alzheimer's disease by administering a test of mental function, like the Montreal Cognitive Assessment (MoCA). The MoCA probes a wide range of cognitive abilities, including language, reasoning, and memory. The Delayed Recall and Verbal Fluency tests that Sister Mary completed are two examples of tasks used in the MoCA. While elderly individuals with no cognitive impairment tend to achieve a score of around twenty-seven out of thirty on the MoCA, people with dementia from Alzheimer's disease score closer to sixteen (Nasreddine et al., 2005).

Sister Mary was one of 678 nuns from the School Sisters of Notre Dame who volunteered for the Nun Study of Aging and Alzheimer's Disease, led by Dr. David Snowdon and colleagues at the University of Minnesota and the University of Kentucky. The goal of this study was to identify social factors that accelerate or impede the onset of dementia. In particular, the investigators were interested in the role of early life education in delaying dementia, given previous reports that individuals with extensive educational backgrounds are more protected against the cognitive symptoms of Alzheimer's disease.

It may seem strange that the study was limited to Catholic nuns, but there are important advantages to this experimental design. Epidemiological studies that examine the relationship between social factors and clinical outcomes can often be difficult to interpret because of the presence of confounding variables. For example, the previously mentioned correlation between early life education and protection against dementia *suggests* that the former causes the latter. But another possible explanation is that people with access to education tend to be wealthier, and wealthy people are more likely to receive consistent medical care, which leads to better health outcomes. While early life education and protection from dementia are correlated, the true relationship between them could be confused since both measures relate to socioeconomic status, a confounding variable.

While statistical methods can help address the confounding problem, the best approach is to study a cohort where subjects are almost identical except for the one variable of interest. Religious groups, like the School Sisters of Notre Dame, present a rare opportunity to conduct a controlled study like this because members of these groups share extremely similar lifestyles. Regardless of their level of education before joining the convent, each sister had the same access to healthcare, living conditions, and diet.

The Nun Study addressed a critical question: what does the brain of a healthy, aged individual like Sister Mary look like? Previous studies focused on individuals diagnosed with Alzheimer's disease, finding fibrous tangles within their brain cells and blocky plaques outside these cells. It was unclear, however, whether these signs of pathology also appear in individuals who never develop the symptoms of Alzheimer's disease.

After her death, the investigators of the Nun Study discovered something surprising about Sister Mary. Each taking their turn to peer through a microscope at slices of her brain, they observed a flood of fibrous tangles and blocky plaques in her hippocampus, a brain structure integral for memory. She had Alzheimer's disease. But she never had dementia. How could someone with significant damage to their brain lack any cognitive impairment?

* * *

An analogy from sports, where resilience to injury is key, might help explain how some individuals can withstand substantial brain damage with no sign of trouble. It is Game Three of the 2021 Eastern Conference Finals, and Giannis Antetokounmpo, a basketball player for the Milwaukee Bucks, is in the air in pursuit of a rebound. He lands awkwardly, with another player on top of him, such that his knee extends thirty degrees beyond its normal range. Writhing on the hardwood floor, you can start to see tears in Giannis' eyes, stemming not only from the excruciating pain, but also from the thought that his season may be over, that his opportunity to lead his team to a championship has vanished.

Physicians who had seen Giannis' injury on television were sure he would be out for the remainder of the playoffs. Another player who suffered a similar but less severe injury missed ten games, more than the number of games left in the season. Remarkably, Giannis missed only two games, returning to lead the Milwaukee Bucks to their first championship in forty years.

How was Giannis able to recover so quickly while others took weeks to return from a similar injury? Giannis is known for his extreme dedication to physical fitness, maintaining a workout routine noted for its intensity even among professional athletes. When asked about his quick return, Giannis' teammates credited his attention to *prehab*, a high level of athleticism before his injury, which aided his ability to perform even if his body was still healing (Reuters, 2021). His extensive training gave him the ability to play basketball even in the presence of structural damage, since his body could compensate for the injury.

In a similar way, one may speculate that Sister Mary's rich educational background prepared her to thrive even in the face of brain damage caused by Alzheimer's disease. By maintaining a high mental fitness over the course of her life, her brain could be thought of as rich in neural resources, such that she could still function even with some of these resources compromised. Neuroscientists use the term *reserve* to refer to these resources, which protect against the cognitive consequences of brain pathology (Cabeza et al., 2018).

Reserve is still a theoretical concept with unclear correspondence to any measurable brain property. But it is thought to be influenced by intellectually engaging endeavors accomplished over a long timeframe, such as education and occupation. Therefore, years of schooling and occupational attainment can be used as proxies for an individual's reserve, explaining the previously reported associations between early life education and protection from the symptoms of Alzheimer's disease.

So what did the Nun Study find? The variable that appeared most predictive of protection from dementia was actually *not* years of childhood education. Recall that this is an imperfect measure of the intellectual engagement that contributes to reserve. Sister Mary, after all, had only eight years of formal schooling, yet a full lifetime of learning. Instead, the researchers made use of old convent records to find a variable that tracked reserve even better.

Shortly after joining the convent, the Sisters of Notre Dame were asked to write autobiographies, describing their lives thus far in intimate detail. Because of the excellent record keeping of the convent, Sisters who were recruited into the Nun Study could find their autobiographies from up to fifty years in the past. These autobiographies allowed researchers to determine if there were clues in those early writings of the eventual cognitive status of the women in old age.

Dr. Snowdon and his colleagues found that the density of ideas contained within the nuns' autobiographies at the age of around twenty-two predicted whether they would develop dementia over fifty years later (Snowdon, 1996). In these early writings, some nuns expressed their ideas in curt, to-the-point phrases, whereas others wrote in more flowery language, packing many thoughts into one sentence. For example, here are a couple of sentences from one of the nuns:

"I was born in Eau Claire, Wis, on May 24, 1913, and was baptized in St James Church."

"Two of the boys are dead."

"'I prefer teaching music to any other profession."

Contrast these phrases to the writings of another nun:

"The happiest day of my life so far was my First Communion Day which was in June nineteen hundred and twenty when I was but eight years of age, and four years later in the same month I was confirmed by Bishop D. D. McGavick."

"Now I am wandering about in 'Dove's Lane' waiting, yet only three more weeks, to follow in the footprints of my Spouse, bound to Him by the Holy Vows of Poverty, Chastity, and Obedience."

Through linguistic analysis of the nuns' writings, each autobiography received a score quantifying the number of ideas expressed per ten words. The latter nun quoted received the highest score, whereas the former received the lowest. Snowdon and colleagues found that individuals with the highest idea density in early life also performed the best on cognitive tests in late life. Furthermore, doctors observed Alzheimer's disease in the brains of individuals with low idea density in early life but not among those who exhibited high idea density in their autobiographies.

The Nun Study demonstrated the importance of early life education in mitigating the effects of Alzheimer's disease in old age. Yet it also suggests that sitting through classes isn't sufficient to benefit from these protective effects. The measures most predictive of dementia prevention were those that directly tracked an individual's linguistic skills at a young age, an ability honed by active engagement with literary material. It's thought that such experiences contribute to an individual's reserve, a theoretical concept that reflects the neural resources a person can rely upon when disease processes damage several brain regions.

* * *

There are two well-researched approaches that both appear to lead to the same goal of preventing dementia from Alzheimer's disease. The first involves lowering the chances of acquiring Alzheimer's disease pathology, marked by the buildup of a protein called beta-amyloid in the brain. Lifestyle factors, such as sleep hygiene, a healthy diet, and exercise, have all been shown to reduce levels of beta-amyloid and diminish the likelihood of acquiring Alzheimer's disease (Crous-Bou et al., 2017).

These lifestyle modifications are helpful not just in preventing dementia but also in improving overall body health, lowering one's chances of suffering other bad outcomes such as a heart attack or diabetes. However, factors outside of one's control, such as genetics, can also influence beta-amyloid buildup. Healthy lifestyle changes alone are not enough to eliminate a person's chance of acquiring Alzheimer's disease.

The second possible approach is to enhance one's cognitive reserve, just as Sister Mary was able to do. While this might not save your brain from Alzheimer's disease pathology, it could prevent dementia, which is the goal that most people are concerned about. According to the Global Council on Brain Health (2017), a group of experts who have extensively reviewed the relevant literature, activities that fulfill and exercise the mind can increase cognitive reserve. For example, lifelong bilingualism, or active use of multiple languages over one's lifetime, has been shown to enhance cognitive reserve and protect individuals from acquiring dementia (Perani et al., 2017).

The Council recommends challenging yourself with cognitively stimulating activities, like playing a favorite musical instrument, to keep the mind healthy and engaged. They also suggest rekindling former hobbies to activate old memories, thus maintaining one's recollection of the past.

Many companies have recently emerged with the intention of designing *brain games* to improve cognitive health in aging individuals. The evidence in favor of brain games is mixed, as the ability for these games to reduce the risk of dementia has not yet been convincingly demonstrated (Global Council on Brain Health, 2017).

"There's a big difference between cognitively engaging activities that you've done and enjoyed for years versus buying a brand-new game which you may not even enjoy playing," said Dr. Jason Karlawish, a geriatrician at the University of Pennsylvania and the author of the book *The Problem of Alzheimer's,* in a conversation we had. The nuance, Dr. Karlawish explains, is that an activity that is done purely as a chore is not necessarily going to be as effective at preserving brain health compared to one intrinsically enjoyed. The advice from the Global Council on Brain Health is to pursue activities that you find challenging but fulfilling, such that you are self-motivated to adhere to them regularly.

A type of cognitive activity often overlooked is social engagement. It comes naturally to some, but carrying a conversation is a complex mental skill that exercises the brain. A lack of social engagement, or social isolation, is associated with an approximately 50 percent increased risk of dementia (National Academies of Sciences, Engineering, and Medicine, 2022). One study found that living alone or participating in few social activities related to structural changes in brain regions affected in Alzheimer's disease, like the hippocampus (Shen et al., 2022).

If you have loved ones who are getting older, it is important that you maintain your connections with them and keep their mind working. As people age, they seek nourishment from their closest relationships and are generally less interested in acquiring new companions (Field and Minkler, 1988). Finding a way to keep people socially engaged is a key goal in the prevention of dementia.

In 2011, researchers estimated that up to half of worldwide cases of dementia related to Alzheimer's disease could be attributed to modifiable risk factors, such as physical inactivity, cognitive inactivity, and obesity (Barnes and Yaffe, 2011). While these are just projections, these findings highlight a couple of important realities. First, interventions to increase cognitive reserve and overall health can certainly help, but they will not eliminate Alzheimer's disease. Plenty of patients buck the trend, succumbing to dementia despite a lifelong career as a sociable college professor.

Nevertheless, we can make tremendous strides in reducing the prevalence of dementia by embracing public health strategies to increase childhood education, encourage healthy diets, and keep seniors cognitively engaged. In fact, we have already made progress. According to the Framingham Heart Study, the risk of dementia has decreased by around 30 percent each decade from the 1970s to 2010s, most likely thanks to improvements in heart health and access to education (Satizabal et al., 2016). We must continue to build on these successes in the 2020s and beyond.

* * *

Much focus has gone toward the development of molecular therapies for Alzheimer's disease. Developing improved treatments for Alzheimer's is an important goal, especially considering that public health interventions will never save everyone from dementia. An effective treatment for Alzheimer's disease could transform the quality of life of millions, justifying the billions of dollars spent toward biomedical research and drug development for this condition. However, the lucrative business of drug development has the potential to corrupt the noble goal of providing better care for patients with Alzheimer's disease.

Many experts fear that the desperation for a novel treatment for Alzheimer's has resulted in the approval of a new drug that lacks convincing clinical benefit. In the summer of 2021, the Food and Drug Administration (FDA) approved a drug called aducanumab, also known as Aduhelm, to be used for the treatment of Alzheimer's disease. This drug, administered by monthly intravenous injections, clears the brain of beta-amyloid, the pathogenic protein thought to be one of the main drivers of brain cell death in Alzheimer's.

Multiple clinical trials testing the efficacy of aducanumab have demonstrated indisputably that the drug is extremely effective at eliminating beta-amyloid from the brain. The FDA cited these results in their decision to approve aducanumab through the *accelerated approval pathway*. This pathway allows therapies effective against an illness's biomarkers to reach patients who otherwise have limited options, even if the drug has yet to show direct clinical benefit.

The original design of the accelerated pathway was to hasten the approval of cancer drugs, which require many decades of study before they can be proven effective since their primary outcome measure is years of survival after diagnosis. The application of this pathway for aducanumab was controversial because the primary outcome measure—slowing of cognitive decline—had already been determined from the clinical trials, and the results were mixed.

Two studies were run to determine aducanumab's effectiveness, and they were both stopped before completion because the drug did not appear to slow cognitive decline. After the trials stopped, however, researchers reanalyzed the data from one of the studies, finding that the patients who received a high dosage of aducanumab exhibited a cognitive decline that was less drastic than those that had received a placebo. The second study did not find the same result. Despite the mixed results, the FDA approved aducanumab because of its proven efficacy against beta-amyloid, the intermediate biomarker that is believed to cause Alzheimer's disease.

Many prominent neurologists have claimed they will not prescribe aducanumab until investigators release more conclusive evidence in support of its clinical efficacy (Grecius and Alexander, 2021). Despite the desperate need for a new treatment, these physicians cite the drug's exorbitant cost and serious side effects as reasons to avoid aducanumab until more clearly establishing its benefits.

The FDA will continue to monitor aducanumab and revisit its approval status if its efficacy remains doubtful after widespread use. As of April 2022, Medicare has decided that it will only cover aducanumab within the context of clinical trials until we learn more about its effectiveness (Belluck, 2022).

If aducanumab is even slightly effective at reducing the toll of Alzheimer's disease, the good that would come cannot be quantified since it would be felt through the eyes of recognition between loved ones, a taken-for-granted warmth that this condition ruthlessly destroys. But until we find a cure, we must not forget the other tools in our arsenal. Because of the 678 nuns from the School Sisters of Notre Dame, we know that dementia is not inevitable. The battle against Alzheimer's disease begins not in old age but rather throughout one's lifespan. During our youthful years, we can start to build the artillery to take down this frightful foe. Therefore, our national response to the growing threat of Alzheimer's should involve not only therapeutic development but also a plan to promote the social factors that led Sister Mary to a long and healthy life.

CHAPTER 8

THE AFTERMATH

$$4x^5 - 4x^4 + 5x^3 - 5x^2 + x - 1 = 0$$

"Find the roots of the equation," says the grinning graduate student, Yu Qiao, eager to see his pupils struggle with the impossible task etched onto the chalkboard. Yu scans the room, surveying the blank faces among the sleep-deprived, scrawny math majors until he spots a raised hand from a friendly-faced man donning over 300 pounds of muscle and wayfarer glasses. John Urschel opens his mouth:

"The roots are 1,± i/2, and ± i"

Yu pauses with astonishment. Finally, he finds words: "How did you solve it?"

Unsure himself, all John can say is that the answer just came to him, like a vision in a dream. An awkward silence settles over the classroom, commemorating the discovery of an uncanny mathematical talent wielded by a man who thought he would dedicate his life to football, a man caught at the intersection of two perpendicular paths.

The conflict between John Urschel's competing interests in math and football speaks to broader concerns relating to the delicate balance between brain health and personal hobbies: a normal topic of conversation between neurologists and their patients but a new one among professional football players.

Was there a person in your high school who seemed to have it all? The soccer team captain who was also the prom queen and boasted a 4.0 GPA? I imagine that John Urschel was a version of that in college. While starring as an offensive lineman on the Penn State football team, he also managed to author several academic publications with titles like *A Space-Time Multigrid Method for the Numerical Variation of Barrier Options* and *Instabilities in the Sun-Jupiter-Asteroid Three Body Problem.*

It is not unheard of for a gifted math major to publish high-quality research papers as an undergraduate. However, to do so while also starting for a powerhouse collegiate football team like Penn State, pancaking enough behemoth nose tackles to punch a ticket to the National Football League (NFL)? In the same year that he earned first-team All-Big Ten honors for his tremendous play as an offensive lineman, he also completed a Master's degree, turning in a thesis that included three publishable papers.

His talents would elevate him to the highest citadels of both his professional endeavors. He would play football in the NFL with the Baltimore Ravens while also studying for a PhD in mathematics at the Massachusetts Institute of Technology (MIT). The decision to do both did not come without tradeoffs.

"Football is a young man's game, but so is math," John notes in his memoir, titled *Mind and Matter: A Life in Math and Football*. "There is a reason that the major award for achievement in mathematics, the Fields Medal, is awarded only to mathematicians under the age of forty."

John's primary concern was that so much time playing football would mean less time doing math. But one must also consider the issue of protecting a gifted brain from a violent sport.

* * *

It is common sense that a major blow to the head is not healthy for the brain. But there are only a few types of head injuries that require immediate medical treatment. To learn what those are, it helps to know three layers of membranes covering the brain: the pia, the arachnoid, and the dura. Collectively, these layers are called the meninges, and they are sandwiched between the brain and the skull, with the pia located closest to the brain and the dura located closest to the skull.

Blood vessels run in and around the layers of the meninges, and these can start bleeding after head trauma. One scary type of injury is called an epidural hematoma. This occurs when an artery between the dura and the skull is damaged and begins to bleed. The patient experiences a brief loss of consciousness, followed by a lucid interval where they are awake and may feel just fine.

Even if a patient thinks they're okay, it is crucial they receive medical care if an epidural hematoma is suspected because a pool of blood could be accumulating inside their skull. The blood eventually puts too much pressure on the brain, causing vital regions that control breathing to stop working, leading to death. The actress Natasha Richardson, who gained fame starring as the mother in *The Parent Trap*, tragically died this way after injuring her head while skiing in Canada (ABC News, 2009).

Another type of injury that is also serious but less of an emergency is called a subdural hemorrhage. This happens when veins between the dura and arachnoid are torn, causing blood to pool underneath the dura. Because blood flow is much slower in veins compared to arteries, subdural hemorrhages grow more gradually compared to epidural hematomas. Since this injury progresses slowly, symptoms may only arise days, weeks, or months after the inciting trauma.

Because these types of injuries increase pressure within the skull, they cause some of the same symptoms seen in Frigyes Karinthy from Chapter two, who had a brain tumor. Those symptoms include worsening headaches, nausea, vomiting, and papillitis—compression of the blood vessels behind the eye. These injuries are diagnosed with a brain scan, which shows a lens-shaped fluid mass if there is an epidural hematoma or a crescent-shaped accumulation of blood if there is a subdural hemorrhage.

The treatment for both injuries is to evacuate the blood from the head by puncturing a hole within the skull, a procedure that a neurosurgeon performs.

Epidural hematomas and subdural hemorrhages are two examples of complications from head trauma that doctors can diagnose from a brain scan and appropriately treat. However, there are other types of head injuries that harm the brain undetected by any of the scans we currently use. One such example is a concussion.

In 2015, the name Terrell Suggs was among the most feared in professional football. An outside linebacker with a PhD in tracking down quarterbacks, he regularly made a fool of offensive linemen like John Urschel, who stood in his way. John didn't have to worry about Suggs embarrassing him during football games. Suggs was a teammate of his on the Baltimore Ravens. However, Suggs slammed into John one day during practice, setting him back in both his football and math careers.

"My memory of what happened next is disjointed," John writes in his memoir. A head collision that causes the brain to shake back and forth in the skull triggers a concussion. This can result in a loss of memory surrounding the event, a change in behavior, and a persistent headache following the injury. While the condition almost always resolves on its own, patients can have trouble concentrating for days, weeks, or months after a concussion.

After his injury, John suffered from a persistent headache, exacerbated by loud sounds and bright lights. The need to shield himself with darkness precluded him from his normal hobbies, like television, surfing the internet, or reading. Every morning, he would take a test that assessed his cognitive function, and his performance was compared to a baseline score he achieved while healthy. It took three weeks until he scored close to normal.

Even after doctors cleared John to resume football, something was still off. He was having trouble remaining productive in math. He was working on a project that would later culminate in a paper titled *On the Characterization and Uniqueness of Centroidal Voronoi Tessellations*, but in the aftermath of his concussion, John struggled to recall theorems crucial for the work. After a few more months, his mathematical skill gradually returned, and he eventually managed to complete the project. Like most people who suffer a concussion, John appeared to make a complete recovery.

Football players are at low risk for epidural hematomas and subdural hemorrhages because they wear helmets that protect their heads from these types of injuries. However, helmets offer only limited protection against other types of head injuries that are more difficult for doctors to visualize, such as concussions. What are the extended effects of these relatively mild head injuries, which don't cause major bleeding but may adversely impact long-term brain health?

* * *

Urschel's career coincided with a sudden realization among the medical community of the risks for neurodegeneration that may accompany professional football. It all started with Mike Webster, a Hall of Fame lineman who spent his final years in deep confusion.

Known to Pittsburgh Steelers fans as Iron Mike for his unparalleled toughness, Webster became profoundly forgetful after retiring from football in 1990. His family noticed a string of strange behaviors following his seventeen-year career. He would wander away from home, only to be found sleeping under a bridge or at the train station. He strapped a pen to his hand with duct tape to keep it from falling as he scribbled thousands of letters. After a streak of poor financial decisions, Mike had trouble finding stable housing, despite the wealth he had previously accumulated playing football. Plagued by several different medical problems, Mike Webster passed away in 2002 from a heart attack he suffered at fifty.

In the morgue where Webster's body was sent worked a neuropathologist from Nigeria named Dr. Bennet Omalu. Curious about the possibility that his history of head trauma related to his mental demise, Dr. Omalu examined Mike's brain in stealth (Laskas, 2016). If his superiors found out what he was doing, he would face repercussions for performing a nonmedically indicated autopsy. But the allure of discovery was too tempting.

Mike's brain looked normal from the outside. There was no evidence of scarring or trauma, contrary to what you might expect from an individual who had sustained multiple serious head injuries. Rather, the pathological changes in Mike's brain were much more subtle, something you could only begin to appreciate if you took out a microscope.

Within the cells of Mike's brain, Dr. Omalu spotted little dark blobs shaped like tadpoles swimming within the matter that once made up the football veteran's consciousness. These tadpoles reflect tau tangles, an essential signature of several neurodegenerative disorders, including Alzheimer's disease.

Dr. Omalu had a strong suspicion of a rare diagnosis for Mike's condition based on the slides of his brain, but he needed confirmation from an esteemed expert. He drove to the University of Pittsburgh with Mike's brain tissue in the trunk, eager to show his former professor, Dr. Ronald Hamilton.

"You're bringing me an Alzheimer's case? You do realize I spend my day with these—" Hamilton began after peering through the microscope at the first couple of slides.

"No, keep looking," Dr. Omalu assured him. Even the well-trained mind jumps first to the most common explanation for a given phenomenon—in this case, Alzheimer's disease-causing tau tangles. Yet a closer look revealed the subtle details of the image, which pointed to an unusual but solid conclusion.

"Huh, so how did you end up with a boxer in that morgue?"

"It's not a boxer."

Chronic traumatic encephalopathy or CTE, as it's more commonly known, was originally called *dementia pugilistica* or punch-drunk syndrome since it was first identified in boxers. This condition afflicted the slugging type of boxers, who embraced a curious strategy. They would tolerate a substantial beating from their opponent in the hopes of eventually landing a knock-out punch. Eventually, these fighters would develop tremors and trouble balancing that onlookers would mistake for the effects of inebriation.

While the medical community was slow to catch on, boxing fans understood this condition for decades. Some fans were concerned for the boxers, urging medical professionals to study the problem. Others would mock the stumbling, confused athletes with insulting jeers like *cuckoo* or *slug nutty*!

Autopsies of the punch-drunk boxers revealed tau tangles affecting several brain regions important for memory and emotion regulation. Dr. Omalu and Dr. Hamilton found evidence of the same pattern of damage in the slides from Mike Webster's brain. The discovery of CTE in a football player triggered an obvious and unsettling question. Might there be other current and former athletes in the NFL also suffering from CTE?

A few years later, another former NFL player received a CTE diagnosis. Then came a watershed study that attracted national attention to the issue. Of 111 NFL players who donated their brains to Dr. Ann McKee's lab at Boston University, 110 of them had CTE (Mez et al., 2017). How did John Urschel react to the publication of this study?

"I was irritated by the way the study's findings were reported by some media outlets, leaving the impression that 99 percent of NFL players have CTE," John writes in his memoir. An astute academic, Urschel was quick to point out that a study like this will have a strong selection bias.

Dr. McKee didn't examine a random sample of NFL players in her 2017 study. Her group analyzed the brains sent to them, referred to them only if the family and doctors caring for the former athlete already suspected CTE. As a result, the cohort in the study did not represent the population of NFL players. While Dr. McKee's article itself is clear on the likelihood of selection bias, these nuances didn't always make their way into the media coverage of the research.

Nevertheless, the study did trigger John to reexamine his life choices. "How could I best serve the talents I was born with? How could I best serve my family and society? What was I willing to risk? What did I hope to gain?" These are questions that patients concerned about neurological disease must always consider, given the brain's central role in all life activities we find meaningful. Oliver Sacks tells a story of a drummer with Tourette's syndrome whose musical talents would soar after his medications wore off (Sacks, 1985). A neurologist treating such a patient must find a treatment plan that preserves the endeavors that provide the person a sense of purpose while also protecting their brain health.

Urschel decided to hang / his helmet and pursue mathematics research full time. The potential of CTE played a role in this decision, but he had already known that nothing could be healthy about a profession where bashing heads with others was a part of the job. More so, John reflected on his opportunity to be a role model to young kids interested in mathematics, especially African-American kids with too few examples of well-known Black mathematicians. He also thought deeply about his potential in academia; how math, like football, rewarded youth, and how his full dedication could provide valuable new insights to the mathematical community.

Dr. John Urschel is currently a mathematician at the Institute for Advanced Study at Princeton, the same establishment where Albert Einstein once worked.

* * *

What is our current understanding of CTE, and how might the ongoing research into this condition help individuals consider their risks of developing it? The first important insight is that this condition does not just affect football athletes. Military veterans, hockey players, and even soccer players can exhibit CTE pathology (Blennow et al., 2016). Contrary to common belief, the risk of CTE does not exactly track the frequency of concussions an individual has experienced over their lifetime. Rather, repeated sub-concussive head injuries have been shown to initiate the disease process that leads to neurodegeneration.

CTE is a diagnosis that can only be made at autopsy, but physicians have recently developed diagnostic guidelines for a related condition in living individuals called traumatic encephalopathy syndrome (Katz et al., 2021). Traumatic encephalopathy syndrome can be diagnosed in a patient with a history of repetitive head impacts who experiences worsening cognitive changes affecting memory, decision-making, and mood. Currently, this diagnosis is primarily used for the purposes of CTE research, but one day it could also help allocate behavioral health resources and treatments to those who need them.

It is important to emphasize that individuals have substantial variability regarding their risk for CTE. Mike Webster's teammate, Terry Bradshaw, had a long career in the NFL, yet you can still find him on television well into his seventies, announcing football games with no signs of cognitive slowing. Just as Sister Mary avoided dementia by keeping an active mind, some studies have suggested that cognitive reserve can also help some individuals avert the long-term consequences of head injuries (Salmond et al., 2006). The prevalence of CTE among professional athletes is still unknown, but it certainly does not affect everyone.

One advance that could alter the way we handle brain injuries clinically would be a brain scan that could monitor mild head trauma. Doctors could use this information to help counsel people about their risk for the possible long-term consequences of repeated brain injury. Severe head trauma leading to bleeding can be detected easily by a computed tomography (CT) scan, but injuries leading to concussion or to CTE evade the imaging techniques routinely administered by doctors. More specialized scans, such as diffusion weighted imaging, could help diagnose mild head injuries by tracking the movement of water in the brain.

What does water movement tell us about brain damage? Head injuries can lead to long-term problems when they affect white matter tracts, the highways of brain communication. Collisions that rotate the head quickly can tear the neural connections within white matter, causing the water normally contained in these tracts to diffuse randomly. This water diffusion does not exactly cause problems, but since it is a sign of neural damage, the phenomenon can give physicians a way to start monitoring head injuries. Diffusion weighted imaging is already used clinically to diagnose some types of brain injury, but its applications could be expanded to detect more subtle signs of head trauma.

Finally, a clear problem is that CTE can only be diagnosed definitively at autopsy. A biomarker for CTE would not only help physicians diagnose patients while they are still living but could also help track damaging pathology in a patient before it becomes a problem.

Early studies have tested the use of PET imaging (discussed in Chapter 3) to identify tau tangles, which are commonly seen in both Alzheimer's disease and CTE (Leuzy et al., 2019). Researchers are also using PET to track the activity of microglia, the resident immune cells of the brain that clear dead tissue after head injury (Coughlin et al., 2017). Just as a physician can monitor a patient's blood pressure and recommend lifestyle changes to prevent a heart attack, it would be extremely useful if a neurologist could discuss an athlete's risk of CTE with similar information.

However, some people will decide they would rather not know their risk of future neurodegeneration, if given the chance. Since there is little we can do to treat the disease, outside of recommending lifestyle adjustments, one could argue there is limited use in knowing, and the psychological impact of such foreknowledge outweighs any potential benefit. Several brain disorders for which we currently lack effective treatments share this concern, including ALS, as discussed in Chapter 5.

After his concussion, John Urschel was asked by a neurologist whether he would like to get a brain scan that could indicate his risk of CTE. His answer?

"I thanked him and said I probably would, but secretly I knew I wouldn't take him up on the offer. The truth was, I did not really want to know."

CHAPTER 9.

REWIRING THE BRAIN

Without any warning, seizures started to haunt Sadie when she was six years old. Normally a happy girl with an infectious laugh, one day, Sadie's father found her staring blankly, inattentive to her surroundings. As soon as her mother came home and held her unresponsive daughter, she called emergency medical services to take them to the hospital. En route to the hospital, Sadie's head began to twitch to the left repeatedly, a tell-tale sign of a seizure.

Aberrant bursts of electrical activity in the brain cause seizures. Brain regions normally communicate with one another using electrical signals, but when there is too much of this activity, a variety of problems can ensue. If you ask the average person to picture a seizure, they will likely describe a scene of an individual uncontrollably shaking their entire body. But this is just one type of seizure, called a convulsive seizure, and it tends to affect the whole brain. Sadie appeared to be having a partial seizure, affecting just the part of her brain that controls head movements and also interrupting her consciousness.

To confirm the type of seizure that Sadie was having, doctors strapped an electroencephalogram (EEG) around her skull at the hospital. The EEG device monitors electrical activity across the whole brain, allowing physicians to pinpoint the region or regions responsible for a seizure. Although Sadie's head twitching stopped in the hospital, the EEG continued to detect low-intensity *subclinical* seizures in her right frontal lobe. These smaller events don't always affect the patient's behavior, but they are a sign that future seizures are waiting to happen.

The most common cause of a seizure is a structural abnormality in the brain, such as a tumor or a stroke. Another potential cause to consider, especially in children, is called cortical dysplasia, which happens when the top layer of the brain does not form properly. An MRI scan of Sadie's brain ruled out all of these possibilities. An infection can also cause seizures, but Sadie didn't look sick, and a test of her spinal fluid showed no signs of such an illness. After two weeks in the hospital, Sadie's doctors sent her home with an array of anti-seizure medications in the hopes of preventing further problems.

Two weeks later, the seizures started again. The blank stare returned as Sadie walked toward the bus with her mom, lasting for about a minute. Despite increasing Sadie's dose of medications at the suggestion of her doctor, her mother observed Sadie's left lip twitching later in the day. Later that month, Sadie received another EEG which showed that the subclinical seizures in her right frontal lobe were happening almost all the time. The doctors informed Sadie and her family that she had drug-resistant epilepsy.

Epilepsy is a seizure disorder diagnosed in patients with at least two or more seizures unprovoked by another condition like a stroke or tumor. Several different disturbances that increase the brain's electrical activity can trigger epilepsy, including genetic mutations that boost neuronal signaling or malformations in brain structure like cortical dysplasia. About two-thirds of patients can control their epilepsy with antiepileptic medications that suppress the brain's predisposition to seizures. The remaining one-third of patients with drug-resistant epilepsy may need to consider more intensive options like neurosurgery to manage their condition.

* * *

It appears likely that the goal of some of the first brain surgeries was to cure epilepsy. In a French burial site, archeologists have uncovered skulls dating back to 6500 BC with holes punched into them, evidence of a procedure called trepanation (Restak, 2000). While we do not fully understand why the ancients bore holes into the skull, we do know that many early cultures believed a buildup of bad spirits in the brain caused seizures (Gross, 1992). Physicians during the Middle Ages also bought into this idea and performed trepanation, hoping to relieve patients of their constant seizures by releasing the evil spirits from the body. It wasn't until the nineteenth century that this approach to epilepsy finally declined in popularity.

As our understanding of epilepsy has grown more scientific, so too has our neurosurgical approach to the disease. The first step in surgically treating epilepsy today is to precisely pinpoint the part of the brain responsible for the seizures. While a normal EEG can point to the right general area, neurosurgeons will implant an EEG device within the skull to identify the exact location in the brain where the seizures originate. By removing just this seizure focus and sparing healthy brain tissue, the surgeon can cure the patient's epilepsy without affecting mental function.

Sadie's case turned out to be more complicated. In the car on the way back from the hospital, her mother recorded a video of her having a new type of seizure. Like the other seizures, her left facial muscles twitch in the video, as her cheek and head jerk to the side. However, this time, Sadie was fully conscious and able to speak during the episode. These episodes also became extremely frequent, happening dozens of times over the next day. Her neurologists immediately recognized this continuous type of seizure as a sign of an inflammatory condition called Rasmussen's encephalitis.

Like multiple sclerosis, Rasmussen's encephalitis results from immune cells infiltrating into the brain. Scientists believe that the immune cells attack special receptors on neurons in this condition, leading to electrical imbalances that cause persistent seizures (Varadker et al., 2014). For unclear reasons, Rasmussen's encephalitis affects just one hemisphere of the brain. Yet it doesn't spare any part of the affected hemisphere, as the inflammation spreads and shrinks the entire half of the brain it chooses.

While anti-inflammatory therapies can slow the damage caused by Rasmussen's, the seizures often persist. If not aggressively handled, the inflammation will cause worsening seizures and cognitive deterioration. The traditional and still widely used approach that can stop the disease from progressing involves removing the entire affected side of the brain, a procedure called a hemispherectomy.

What seems to be a miracle is that very young children who have half of their brain removed can remain highly functional. This is thanks to the brain's incredible plasticity. After Sadie received the diagnosis, her mom did a video call with the mother of a child who received a hemispherectomy around the age of three. While her twenty-year-old son still has challenges controlling the right half of his body, he can walk, speak, and has even been able to graduate from high school and attend college.

However, the brain loses much of its plasticity by a child's sixth birthday, meaning that the removal of Sadie's right hemisphere could have a dramatic effect. She would be expected to lose sight and hearing from her left eye or ear, as well as her ability to move her left arm or leg. The logic behind such an aggressive treatment is to completely stop the seizures, which not only reduce the patient's quality of life but can also cause severe brain damage and irreversible cognitive changes. But what if there is another way to prevent the seizures without removing so much brain tissue?

Sadie's parents begged for other options, writing in to Dr. Lisa Sanders' column *Diagnosis* to crowd-source readers of the *New York Times* to explore alternative diagnoses or treatments. Sadie's story clearly struck a nerve. Video responses flooded into her mother's inbox, and some were shown in a documentary series later released by *Netflix* also titled *Diagnosis*. Most readers acknowledged that Rasmussen's encephalitis was the most likely diagnosis. But some proposed a different treatment, one that relies on portable technology.

The Neuropace RNS (Responsive NeuroStimulation) system is a device implanted directly onto the brain designed to sense and stop seizures. It monitors the brain's electrical activity in the same way that an EEG does. Once it detects that a seizure is about to happen, it delivers electrical stimulation to the appropriate area to correct the aberrant activity. Like a pacemaker for the brain, the device helps people with drug-resistant epilepsy live more autonomously, without the constant possibility of a seizure.

"I couldn't drive. I couldn't go out on my own," explained Michelle, a sixty-seven-year-old woman interviewed by WFAA, a local news channel in Texas. She would endure hundreds of seizures per day before the Neuropace RNS device finally controlled her epilepsy. Now she only has two to three mild seizures a day, allowing her to travel and exercise in a way that was previously not possible.

For patients like Sadie, an especially attractive feature of the Neuropace device is that it does not require the removal of any part of the brain. The prevention of her seizures can allow her brain to develop healthily, preserving crucial brain tissue that would otherwise become badly damaged over years of chaotic brain activity.

The Neuropace RNS is just one example of a brain-computer interface (BCI), a term that generally refers to technologies that translate information from brain activity into actionable outputs to assist human functioning. Brain-computer interfaces were first popularized for their application in limb prosthetics for individuals paralyzed by spinal cord injuries. A BCI can detect someone's *intention* to move their arm, for example, by measuring electrical activity in the motor control center of the brain. Then it can send signals to a robotic arm attached to the patient to move the limb in the direction and force intended by the user.

What started as a technology to help patients navigate the physical world has now enabled them to explore the digital.

"hello world! Short tweet. Monumental progress."

"no need for keystrokes or voices. I created this tweet just by thinking it. #helloworldbci"

"my hope is that I'm paving the way for people to tweet through their thoughts phil"

These tweets from the Australian neurologist Thomas Oxley's Twitter account came not from Dr. Oxley but from his patient, Phil (TED, 2022). Like Rebecca from Chapter 5, Phil has ALS, and his condition has progressed to the point that he has lost control over most of his muscles. Instead of Rebecca's Tobii Dynavox eye-tracking system, Phil can communicate through Stentrode, a Bluetooth device implanted in his brain. Similar to the thrombectomy procedure described in Chapter 1, the Stentrode is placed into the brain by a doctor who threads the device up through a vein in the neck. Once it's inside, the BCI can record Phil's brain activity, granting him control over other devices like his smartphone.

Clearly, the applications of BCIs are wide-ranging and impressive. There are reasons, however, for why brain-computer interfaces are not currently available to everyone who may benefit from them, and they are not just related to cost. After implantation into the brain, BCIs require periodic maintenance like the replacement of a battery or repositioning. Research is still ongoing on how to make these devices more durable, capable of lasting for years without compromising quality.

One must also understand that brain-computer interfaces require a lengthy period of calibration with the user to associate brain signals with the desired output. After her family carefully considered all of their options, Sadie received the Neuropace RNS device. The device did not, and was not designed to cure her symptoms immediately. Her Neuropace first needed to learn what her seizures looked like so that it could provide therapeutic stimulation only when necessary.

It has now been a couple of years since Sadie's operation. From an Instagram account maintained by her mother, it is apparent that she has been able to return to school and enjoy outdoor activities like strawberry picking and scooter rides on the boardwalk. Her outlook would have looked much different had her seizures continued to cause damage to her brain or if her right hemisphere had been surgically removed.

* * *

Brain-computer interfaces are different from other therapeutic interventions. They augment human capacities as if they are granting a person a new sense or physical ability. What are the consequences of this arguably superhuman transformation?

Rita Leggett was forty-nine years old when a surgeon placed a device called NeuroVista in her brain to control her epilepsy. NeuroVista works a bit differently than Neuropace. Both machines detect whether the patient will soon have a seizure, but while Neuropace corrects the aberrant activity, NeuroVista alerts the patient so that they can prepare for the event. Like the Stentrode device, NeuroVista communicates wirelessly to an external unit that fits in the patient's pocket and beeps and flashes around fifteen minutes before a seizure.

The NeuroVista alerts helped Rita manage her condition adeptly. She was first alerted while at the hairdresser. A flashing light from the external unit prompted her to take her medications and go home, thus avoiding the commotion of having a seizure in public. Collaborating with a machine in such a way felt strange at first, but eventually, it became natural. In a 2017 interview she would later give with the *New Yorker,* she explained: "We were calibrated together. We became one."

Rita was happy with her device. But three years after her neurosurgeons had implanted the device, they needed to go back and remove it. NeuroVista had run out of funding, and the company would no longer be available to repair Rita's device if it ever broke down. For Rita, the BCI had become integrated into her identity. When it was taken away, she wrestled with a deep incompleteness, as if her sense of balance had been stolen.

It is not uncommon for people to have deeply personal experiences with the devices that inhabit them. Frederic Gilbert is a philosopher who has studied Rita and others like her who have interacted with brain-computer interfaces. The subjective experience of having a device implanted in your brain is commonly overlooked in academic journals that initially publish these procedures, yet Gilbert's research has shown these experiences can have effects on one's personhood.

Many of the subjects he interviewed reported that they were a totally different person after the procedure (Gilbert et al., 2017). Some acquired a newfound confidence, feeling empowered by their control over a condition that previously limited their freedom. Other patients had the opposite experience, sharing that the frequent interventions constantly reminded them of their condition. As they continued to see the device as *other*, the brain-computer interface compromised their autonomy and undermined their confidence.

Medical procedures that appear to *fix* a brain problem don't always have their intended effect. Oliver Sacks once described a patient who was blind for most of his childhood and adult life due to cataracts until he received a surgery that restored his ability to see (Sacks, 1995). One might think such a transformation would be empowering, but Sacks's patient found his newly acquired vision profoundly disorienting, like a bright flashing light that distracted him constantly. In fact, he was relieved when his cataracts and blindness returned. If the brain has already learned to interpret the world with sound, touch, and smell, then adding a new sense just makes things more confusing.

"Brain-computer interfaces are ultimately going to enable a passage of information that goes beyond the limitations of the human body," said Dr. Oxley in a 2022 interview with the *New York Times*. Since it can be difficult to anticipate whether individuals will react positively or negatively to the addition of new abilities, it is important that all procedures in this space are performed with consent and are reversible. Informed consent can be difficult to obtain when patients are receiving such devices to communicate more easily in the first place, yet it is a crucial step for BCIs to be introduced into society ethically.

Ethical considerations abound, but brain-computer interfaces will likely make their way to the patients who need them eventually. One of the most valuable gifts that doctors can provide for patients is the opportunity to regain control over their body and their life. BCIs can offer patients such autonomy, so there will always be demand.

The best treatment is prevention, but prevention is not always possible. Diseases like epilepsy are often caused by unpredictable events, such as random genetic mutations or deviations in brain development. Nevertheless, there are ways in which doctors can handle conditions like epilepsy proactively. Since seizures can cause long-term and irreversible brain damage, it is essential that they are identified and managed early.

A good friend of mine has Type 1 Diabetes. He wears a device called an insulin pump, which continuously monitors his glucose levels, and automatically injects insulin if his blood sugar gets too high. "If I were born one hundred years ago, before the discovery of insulin, I wouldn't be alive," he once said to me, reflecting on his good luck in life. The insulin pump provides him the same control over his condition that many patients with epilepsy desire to have over theirs. Technologies like the Neuropace RNS device, which also reacts to a bodily abnormality and delivers the antidote, can finally offer this.

CONCLUSION

As I write this final chapter on my laptop, I glance to the top right of the screen and click on the battery sign to see how much time I have before I need to find a charger. I spot a familiar symbol—a yellow triangle with an exclamation mark embedded inside, along with the clarifying text: "Service Recommended." I should really take the laptop to the Apple store and get the battery replaced, I realize. But I am so busy—when do I have the time to do that? Plus the laptop has been working just fine. I'll take it to the store once I notice a problem.

And herein lies the fundamental obstacle to the vision described in this book.

The concept of going to see a doctor when one is healthy is fairly unintuitive. We don't call the plumber when the shower *is* working, nor do we want to talk to a lawyer unless we have legal problems. This logic is a major reason why so many people are hesitant to take vaccines, medications almost always administered to healthy people. Why should I go out of my way to see a doctor when I'm likely going to be safe from any severe consequences?

"You are absolutely correct that there are risks to getting the COVID-19 vaccine. Every medical procedure that we perform involves some level of risk." Beneath two layers of blue face masks, I rehearsed this dialogue with a triple-vaccinated actor donning an N95, who is pretending to be a vaccine-hesitant patient for our class on "Doctoring" etiquette.

"But there are also risks associated with not getting vaccinated. And those risks, unfortunately, include some pretty serious potential consequences, such as severe illness, hospitalization, or death." Despite the contrived nature of my conversation with this fully vaccinated professional, it allowed me to meditate on an important idea: just as there are costs and consequences to any given *action*, there are also costs and consequences to any *inaction*.

The potential costs of failing to prevent brain disorders are very high. As described in this book, diseases of the mind can rob a person of their most vital skills, impeding their ability to live the life they want. So let us recap what we can do now to reduce our chances of acquiring a brain disorder and what we may be able to do in the future to avoid such a fate.

Good research indicates that dementia is preventable by remaining stimulated cognitively throughout life, keeping a consistent sleep schedule, and maintaining a healthy, active lifestyle. These practices reduce the levels of destructive proteins in your brain and prepare your brain to withstand damage should it occur. We also learned about the role of head injuries, not just major ones but also repeated minor head collisions, in causing irreversible cognitive changes.

You can remember another crucial lesson with the acronym FAST: if you see a person experience sudden Facial drooping, Arm weakness, or Speech difficulties, it is Time to call emergency services because they could be having a stroke. Stroke is a good example of a brain condition where early identification and treatment can lead to excellent outcomes since doctors can administer therapies that stop the stroke before it causes too much damage.

We also discussed brain disorders where a preventive approach is currently infeasible due to a lack of known modifiable risk factors. These include brain tumors, epilepsy, and multiple sclerosis. The way forward for conditions like these will involve proactive approaches, which might not eliminate the disease altogether, but can prevent it from getting worse. Scientists have developed several proactive treatments for these diseases, including CAR-T cell therapies, brain-computer interfaces, and stem cell transplantations. And there is hope for a truly preventive approach for multiple sclerosis, in the form of a vaccine against its causative agent, the Epstein-Barr Virus.

Finally, an elusive tool that could improve our ability to treat brain disease is a biomarker for the mind, a "stethoscope" that would allow doctors to monitor a patient's brain health. A stethoscope for the brain can take many forms—it could be a brain scan that identifies early signs of Parkinson's disease, a blood assay for inflammatory chemicals that affect mood, a DNA test for an unfortunate predictor of ALS. A tool like this can help doctors start treatments earlier, leading to better outcomes for patients.

* * *

"I think we have been fooled about what we can expect from medicine—fooled, one could say, by penicillin," writes Atul Gawande in *The Checklist Manifesto*. A miracle drug of the early twentieth century, penicillin was the first recognized antibiotic, capable of treating a spectacular range of infectious illnesses. Since the discovery of antibiotics, doctors have hoped that every human disease could be neutralized by an appropriate drug—a cure for cancer, a silver bullet for diabetes. It turned out that not even penicillin could fulfill the promise of penicillin, as many infectious agents soon became resistant to its powers. Nevertheless, we have still managed to claim victory over most of the pathogens that surround us by washing our hands, cooking our food, and drinking clean water.

Simple lifestyle practices can protect our brains from disease, although healthy living is not always enough. It is also clear that new treatments can help patients manage their condition, but will not eliminate every malady of the mind. What is needed is to populate the in-between space, where medicine and daily living interact. Just as colonoscopies and Pap Smears are recognized as common practices that one should schedule regularly, we need similar types of tests for brain health.

I wish that this could be a self-help book, where I could provide a list of practical suggestions to protect every mind from disease. While I have pointed to some practices that could help, the truth is that we need more research into how we can track and modify brain conditions before they occur. Several challenges impede our progress, and not all of them are biomedical in nature. Improving access to health care, protecting young children from neglect, increasing the availability of healthy foods—it is crucial that we also address public policy goals like these to realize the vision set forward in this book.

The good news is that a lot of the hard work has already been done for us. We stand on the shoulders of giants in medicine, physicians and scientists of the past who have painstakingly described and characterized the maladies of the mind. Now that we can diagnose brain diseases and predict their course, we must learn how to stop these stealthy thieves in their tracks.

ACKNOWLEDGMENTS

Like peeling an onion, I must thank several concentric spheres of people for their indispensable support in creating the book in your hands. Like chopping an onion, there may be a tear or two shed—don't tell anyone.

Starting with the outermost sphere, the publication of this book relied on funds generously raised by a community of early supporters during a presale campaign. I have no words that will appropriately express my gratitude for your invaluable contributions to this product. The names of each supporter are at the end of this section. I hope I have delivered a book that will make you proud.

In the next sphere, I thank the beta readers who gave spectacular feedback that improved the manuscript ten-fold. Thank you, Ananya, Amit, Diane, Gyan, Cooper, Ellie, Keshav, Jason, Yonatan, and Emily, for looking over chapters and sharing your thoughts. I cannot give enough thanks to Likhitha, who has seen countless drafts of multiple chapters and provided the most helpful feedback that I have ever received on anything I have worked on. Your Microsoft Word comments to "Add more details!" will haunt me in my sleep.

The third sphere contains the team of editors and mentors I have worked with at The Creator's Institute and New Degree Press, who provided an infrastructure and support network that made the book publication process much smoother than I could have anticipated. Thank you to my editors, Trisha and Mozelle, for keeping me accountable with this book over the course of a year. Of course, none of this would have been possible without Professor Eric Koester, who has created an innovative program that has welcomed so many new voices into the publishing arena.

Next, I thank my professors who have contributed to the book both directly through conversations we've shared, or indirectly, through teaching me all I know about medicine and the brain. Thank you specifically to Jason Karlawish, Sara Manning Peskin, and Lisa Sanders, who generously lent me their time and their thoughts as I figured out the scope, focus, and content of the book.

The innermost sphere, quite ironically, encompasses the most amount of people. At its core, this book is for the patients and families who live with brain disease. To those who have spoken to the world or to me directly about your condition, thank you for sharing your stories so openly and so honestly, such that others may benefit. This book can only be considered a success if it sparks new advances in research and patient care.

Thank you again to my Author Community who provided early support for this work: Adam Kamboj, Ajay Virmani, Ajoy Nayak, Amira Kamboj, Amit Mandal, Ananya Mandal, Anchith Kota, Anjana Saha, Annette Racaniello, Basabi Virmani, Brandon Aurigema, Carl Lubin, Cheli Lange, Chetan Virmani, Chitto Saha, Chris Sennett, David Kochummen, Diane Rafizadeh, Eliana Rosenthal, Emily Lubin, Eric Koester, Felix Caceres, Glynnis Dwelly, Gyan Moorthy, Haley Cohen, Hannah Kotz, Henry Greene, Ilinca Butnariu, James Paslay, Jayanta Mandal, Jhuma Kamboj, Jon Kanen, Julianna Russo, Kareem Kamboj, Kathy Lubin, Lakshmi Kolla, Likhitha Kolla, Luke Cooke, Manoj Trehan, Mary Menaquale, Michael Dingamadji, Mousumi Shaw, Neeru Kumar, Nilesh Virmani, Partha Chatterjee, Partha Choudhury, Peda Babu Kandru, Prabir Biswas, Priyanka Virmani, Purabi Mandal, Raja Varma, Reeta Majumdar, Reshmi Palit, Sanjeev Nath, Saptarshi Mukherjee, Sara Manning, Sarah Garcia, Sarbananda Guharoy, Seema Nambiar, Soma Saha, Steven Brem, Subba Rao Kolla, Sugata Bagchi, Tank Lubin, Tara Balasubramanian, Timothy Green, Tim Jean, William Das, Yonatan Babore, and Zach Gardner.

APPENDIX

INTRODUCTION:

Sacks, Oliver. *The Man Who Mistook His Wife for a Hat: And Other Clinical Tales*. New York: Summit Books, 1985.

CHAPTER 1:

Dronkers, N. F., O. Plaisant, M. T. Iba-Zizen, and E. A. Cabanis. "Paul Broca's Historic Cases: High Resolution MR Imaging of the Brains of Leborgne and Lelong." *Brain* 130, no. 5 (2007): 1432–41. https://doi.org/10.1093/brain/awm042.

Gajardo-Vidal, Andrea, Diego L. Lorca-Puls, PLORAS team, Holly Warner, Bawan Pshdary, Jennifer T. Crinion, Alexander P. Leff, et al. "Damage to Broca's Area Does Not Contribute to Long-Term Speech Production Outcome after Stroke." *Brain* 144, no. 3 (2021): 817–32. https://doi.org/10.1093/brain/awaa460.

Lorch, Marjorie. "Re-Examining Paul Broca's Initial Presentation of M. Leborgne: Understanding the Impetus for Brain and Language Research." *Cortex* 47, no. 10 (2011): 1228–35. https://doi.org/10.1016/j.cortex.2011.06.022.

Mohammed, Nasser, Vinayak Narayan, Devi Prasad Patra, and Anil Nanda. "Louis Victor Leborgne ('Tan')." *World*

Neurosurgery 114 (2018): 121–25. https://doi.org/10.1016/j. wneu.2018.02.021.

Sondhaus, Elizabeth, and Stanley Finger. "Aphasia and the CNS from Imhotep to Broca." *Neuropsychology* 2, no. 2 (1988): 87–110. https://doi.org/10.1037/h0091739.

CHAPTER 2:

Bassett, Danielle Smith, and Ed Bullmore. "Small-World Brain Networks." *The Neuroscientist* 12, no. 6 (2006): 512–23. https://doi.org/10.1177/1073858406293182.

Dandy, Walter E. "Removal of Right Cerebral Hemisphere for Certain Tumors with Hemiplegia." *Journal of the American Medical Association* 90, no. 11 (1928): 823. https://doi.org/10.1001/jama.1928.02690380007003.

Karinthy, Frigyes. *A Journey Round My Skull: Transl. from the Hungarian by Vernon Duckwerth Barker. 3. IMPR.* London, 1939.

Majzner, Robbie G., Sneha Ramakrishna, Kristen W. Yeom, Shabnum Patel, Harshini Chinnasamy, Liora M. Schultz, Rebecca M. Richards, et al. "GD2-Car T Cell Therapy for H3K27M-Mutated Diffuse Midline Gliomas." *Nature* 603, no. 7903 (2022): 934–41. https://doi.org/10.1038/s41586-022-04489-4.

Mandal, Ayan S., Rafael Romero-Garcia, Michael G. Hart, and John Suckling. "Genetic, Cellular, and Connectomic Characterization of the Brain Regions Commonly Plagued by Glioma." *Brain* 143, no. 11 (2020): 3294–3307. https://doi.org/10.1093/brain/awaa277.

Mukherjee, Siddhartha. *The Emperor of All Maladies: A Biography of Cancer.* New York: Scribner, 2011.

CHAPTER 3:

"Actor Michael J. Fox Has Parkinson's Disease." *Washington Post*. WP Company, November 26, 1998. https://www. washingtonpost.com/archive/lifestyle/1998/11/26/actor-michael-j-fox-has-parkinsons-disease/6ec9ab0e-53a6-479f-973f-f9fc64e568f9/.

Bethlehem, R.A.I., Seidlitz, J., White, S.R. *et al*. Brain charts for the human lifespan. *Nature* 604, 525–533 (2022). https://doi. org/10.1038/s41586-022-04554-y.

Egan, Elisabeth. "When It Comes to Living with Uncertainty, Michael J. Fox Is a Pro." *New York Times*. The New York Times, November 13, 2020. https://www.nytimes.com/2020/11/13/ books/michael-j-fox-no-time-like-the-future.html.

Fox, Michael J. *No Time like the Future: An Optimist Considers Mortality*. New York, N.Y: Flatiron Books, 2020.

Freeman, Hadley. "Michael J Fox: 'Every Step Now Is a Frigging Math Problem, so I Take It Slow'." *The Guardian*. Guardian News and Media, November 21, 2020. https://www.theguardian.com/culture/2020/nov/21/michael-j-fox-every-step-now-is-a-frigging-math-problem-so-i-take-it-slow.

Holly Teichholtz, Chief Marketing Officer. "Breaking News: Critical Advance Announced in Imaging the Living Parkinson's Brain." The Michael J. Fox Foundation for Parkinson's Research | Parkinson's Disease. Accessed May 25, 2022. https://www.michaeljfox.org/news/breaking-news-critical-advance-announced-imaging-living-parkinsons-brain.

Marras, C., J. C. Beck, J. H. Bower, E. Roberts, B. Ritz, G. W. Ross, R. D. Abbott, et al. "Prevalence of Parkinson's Disease across North America." *npj Parkinson's Disease* 4, no. 1 (2018). https:// doi.org/10.1038/s41531-018-0058-0.

CHAPTER 4:

"Adverse Childhood Experiences." Let's Get Healthy California, February 1, 2022. https://letsgethealthy.ca.gov/goals/healthy-beginnings/adverse-childhood-experiences/.

Aristotle, A. L. Peck. "Parts of Animals, with an English Translation by A. L. Peck." Harvard, Cambridge, 1955. https://doi.org/10.5962/bhl.title.30408.

Bullmore, Edward T. *The Inflamed Mind: A Radical New Approach to Depression.* New York: Picador, 2019.

Cheong, E. Von, Carol Sinnott, Darren Dahly, and Patricia M. Kearney. "Adverse Childhood Experiences (ACES) and Later-Life Depression: Perceived Social Support as a Potential Protective Factor." *BMJ Open* 7, no. 9 (2017). https://doi.org/10.1136/bmjopen-2016-013228.

Felitti, Vincent J., Robert F. Anda, Dale Nordenberg, David F. Williamson, Alison M. Spitz, Valerie Edwards, Mary P. Koss, and James S. Marks. "Relationship of Childhood Abuse and Household Dysfunction to Many of the Leading Causes of Death in Adults." *American Journal of Preventive Medicine* 14, no. 4 (1998): 245–58. https://doi.org/10.1016/s0749-3797(98)00017-8.

Gross, Charles G. "Aristotle on the Brain." *The Neuroscientist* 1, no. 4 (1995): 245–50. https://doi.org/10.1177/107385849500100408.

Iob, Eleonora, and Andrew Steptoe. "Adverse Childhood Experiences, Inflammation, and Depressive Symptoms in Later Life: A Prospective Cohort Study." *The Lancet* 394 (2019). https://doi.org/10.1016/s0140-6736(19)32855-7.

Lacey, Rebecca E., Snehal M. Pinto Pereira, Leah Li, and Andrea Danese. "Adverse Childhood Experiences and Adult Inflammation: Single Adversity, Cumulative Risk and Latent Class Approaches." *Brain, Behavior, and Immunity* 87 (2020): 820–30. https://doi.org/10.1016/j.bbi.2020.03.017.

Lee, Chieh-Hsin, and Fabrizio Giuliani. "The Role of Inflammation in Depression and Fatigue." *Frontiers in Immunology* 10 (2019). https://doi.org/10.3389/fimmu.2019.01696.

National Rheumatoid Arthritis Society. "Invisible disease: rheumatoid arthritis and chronic fatigue." London, 2014.

"Take the Ace Quiz – and Learn What It Does and Doesn't Mean." Center on the Developing Child at Harvard University, May 30, 2019. https://developingchild.harvard.edu/media-coverage/take-the-ace-quiz-and-learn-what-it-does-and-doesnt-mean/#:~:text=An%20ACE%20score%20is%20a,quotes%20Center%20Director%20Jack%20P.

"Understanding Depression in All Its Complexity—Gates Cambridge." Gates Cambridge, December 9, 2021. https://www.gatescambridge.org/about/news/understanding-depression-in-all-its-complexity/

CHAPTER 5:

Bauby, Jean-Dominique. *The Diving Bell and the Butterfly: A Memoir of Life in Death*. New York: Random House, 1998.

Tran, Hélène, Michael P. Moazami, Huiya Yang, Diane McKenna-Yasek, Catherine L. Douthwright, Courtney Pinto, Jake Metterville, et al. "Suppression of Mutant C9ORF72 Expression by a Potent Mixed Backbone Antisense Oligonucleotide." *Nature Medicine* 28, no. 1 (2021): 117–24. https://doi.org/10.1038/s41591-021-01557-6.

CHAPTER 6:

Bjornevik, Kjetil, Marianna Cortese, Brian C. Healy, Jens Kuhle, Michael J. Mina, Yumei Leng, Stephen J. Elledge, et al. "Longitudinal Analysis Reveals High Prevalence of Epstein-Barr Virus Associated with Multiple Sclerosis." *Science* 375, no. 6578 (2022): 296–301. https://doi.org/10.1126/science.abj8222.

Craven, Caroline. "Selma Blair Undergoing Stem Cell Treat-
    ments for Multiple Sclerosis." Healthline. Healthline Media,
    July 31, 2019. https://www.healthline.com/health-news/
    actress-selma-blair-undergoing-stem-cell-treatment-for-mul-
    tiple-sclerosis#What-researchers-know-about-HSCT.

Good Morning America. "Selma Blair Cried with Relief at MS
    Diagnosis after Being 'Not Taken Seriously'." Good Morning
    America. February 26, 2019. Accessed May 28, 2022. https://
    www.goodmorningamerica.com/culture/story/selma-blair-
    opens-tears-relief-ms-diagnosis-61310469.

Good Morning America. "Selma Blair Talks about Living with
    MS, Her Recovery after Stem Cell Treatment." Good Morning
    America. Accessed May 28, 2022. https://www.goodmornin-
    gamerica.com/news/video/selma-blair-talks-living-ms-re-
    covery-stem-cell-80531324.

"Introducing, Selma Blair." Discovery. Accessed May 28, 2022.
    https://www.discovery.com/shows/introducing-selma-blair.

Lanz, Tobias V., R. Camille Brewer, Peggy P. Ho, Jae-Seung Moon,
    Kevin M. Jude, Daniel Fernandez, Ricardo A. Fernandes, et
    al. "Clonally Expanded B Cells in Multiple Sclerosis Bind EBV
    EBNA1 and GlialCAM." *Nature* 603, no. 7900 (2022): 321–27.
    https://doi.org/10.1038/s41586-022-04432-7.

"Moderna Announces First Participant Dosed in Phase 1 Study
    of Its Mrna Epstein-Barr Virus (EBV) Vaccine." Accessed
    May 28, 2022. https://investors.modernatx.com/news/
    news-details/2022/Moderna-Announces-First-Participant-
    Dosed-in-Phase-1-Study-of-its-mRNA-Epstein-Barr-Virus-
    EBV-Vaccine/default.aspx.

Muraro, Paolo A., Roland Martin, Giovanni Luigi Mancardi,
    Richard Nicholas, Maria Pia Sormani, and Riccardo Saccardi.
    "Autologous Haematopoietic Stem Cell Transplantation for

Treatment of Multiple Sclerosis." *Nature Reviews Neurology* 13, no. 7 (2017): 391–405. https://doi.org/10.1038/nrneurol.2017.81.

Stump, Scott. "Selma Blair Walks Red Carpet with Special Monogrammed Cane after MS Diagnosis." TODAY.com. TODAY, February 25, 2019. https://www.today.com/popculture/selma-blair-walks-red-carpet-special-monogrammed-cane-after-ms-t149344.

The View. "Selma Blair on Why She Was Relieved after MS Diagnosis: 'I Was Never Believed' | the View." YouTube. YouTube, May 19, 2022. https://www.youtube.com/watch?v=i-flXLznCDwE.

"What Are the Risk Factors for Lung Cancer?" Centers for Disease Control and Prevention. Centers for Disease Control and Prevention, October 18, 2021. https://www.cdc.gov/cancer/lung/basic_info/risk_factors.htm#:~:text=People%20who%20smoke%20cigarettes%20are,the%20risk%20of%20lung%20cancer.

CHAPTER 7:

Barnes, Deborah E., and Kristine Yaffe. "The Projected Effect of Risk Factor Reduction on Alzheimer's Disease Prevalence." *The Lancet Neurology* 10, no. 9 (2011): 819–28. https://doi.org/10.1016/s1474-4422(11)70072-2.

Belluck, Pam. "Medicare Officially Limits Coverage of Aduhelm to Patients in Clinical Trials." *New York Times*. The New York Times, April 7, 2022. https://www.nytimes.com/2022/04/07/health/aduhelm-medicare-alzheimers.html.

Cabeza, Roberto, Marilyn Albert, Sylvie Belleville, Fergus I. Craik, Audrey Duarte, Cheryl L. Grady, Ulman Lindenberger, et al. "Maintenance, Reserve and Compensation: The Cognitive Neuroscience of Healthy Ageing." *Nature Reviews*

Neuroscience 19, no. 11 (2018): 701–10. https://doi.org/10.1038/ s41583-018-0068-2.

Crous-Bou, Marta, Carolina Minguillón, Nina Gramunt, and José Luis Molinuevo. "Alzheimer's Disease Prevention: From Risk Factors to Early Intervention." *Alzheimer's Research & Therapy* 9, no. 1 (2017). https://doi.org/10.1186/s13195-017-0297-z.

"FDA Grants Accelerated Approval for Alzheimer's Drug." US Food and Drug Administration. FDA. Accessed May 28, 2022. https://www.fda.gov/news-events/press-announcements/ fda-grants-accelerated-approval-alzheimers-drug.

Field, D., and M. Minkler. "Continuity and Change in Social Support between Young-Old and Old-Old or Very-Old Age." *Journal of Gerontology* 43, no. 4 (1988). https://doi.org/10.1093/ geronj/43.4.p100.

Global Council on Brain Health. "Engage Your Brain: GCBH Recommendations on Cognitively Stimulating Activities." 2017. www.GlobalCouncilOnBrainHealth.org.

Greicius, Michael, and G. Caleb Alexander. "People Want an Alzheimer's Drug. This Isn't the One." *New York Times*. The New York Times, May 28, 2021. https://www.nytimes. com/2021/05/28/opinion/alzheimer-treatment-FDA-adu-canumab.html.

Nasreddine, Ziad S., Natalie A. Phillips, Valerie Bedirian, Simon Charbonneau, Victor Whitehead, Isabelle Collin, Jeffrey L. Cummings, and Howard Chertkow. "The Montreal Cognitive Assessment, MOCA: A Brief Screening Tool for Mild Cognitive Impairment." *Journal of the American Geriatrics Society* 53, no. 4 (2005): 695–99. https://doi.org/10.1111/j.1532-5415.2005.53221.x.

National Academies of Sciences, Engineering, and Medicine. "Social Isolation and Loneliness in Older Adults." 2020. https://doi.org/10.17226/25663.

Perani, Daniela, Mohsen Farsad, Tommaso Ballarini, Francesca Lubian, Maura Malpetti, Alessandro Fracchetti, Giuseppe Magnani, Albert March, and Jubin Abutalebi. "The Impact of Bilingualism on Brain Reserve and Metabolic Connectivity in Alzheimer's Dementia." *Proceedings of the National Academy of Sciences* 114, no. 7 (2017): 1690–95. https://doi.org/10.1073/pnas.1610909114.

Reuters. "Bucks' Giannis Feared He Could Be 'Out a Year' after Knee Injury." INQUIRER.net, July 7, 2021. https://sports.inquirer.net/427970/bucks-giannis-feared-he-could-be-out-a-year-after-knee-injury.

Satizabal, Claudia L., Alexa S. Beiser, Vincent Chouraki, Geneviève Chêne, Carole Dufouil, and Sudha Seshadri. "Incidence of Dementia over Three Decades in the Framingham Heart Study." *New England Journal of Medicine* 374, no. 6 (2016): 523–32. https://doi.org/10.1056/nejmoa1504327.

Shen, Chun, Edmund Rolls, Wei Cheng, Jujiao Kang, Guiying Dong, Chao Xie, Xing-Ming Zhao, Barbara Sahakian, and Jianfeng Feng. "Associations of Social Isolation and Loneliness with Later Dementia." *Neurology*, 2022. https://doi.org/10.1212/wnl.0000000000200583.

Snowdon, D. A. "Aging and Alzheimer's Disease: Lessons from the Nun Study." *The Gerontologist* 37, no. 2 (1997): 150–56. https://doi.org/10.1093/geront/37.2.150.

Snowdon, David. *Aging with Grace: The Nun Study and the Science of Old Age: How We Can All Live Longer, Healthier and More Vital Lives.* London: Fourth Estate, 2008.

Snowdon, David A. "Linguistic Ability in Early Life and Cognitive Function and Alzheimer's Disease in Late

Life." *JAMA* 275, no. 7 (1996): 528. https://doi.org/10.1001/
jama.1996.03530310034029.

"The Global Council on Brain Health (GCBH)." AARP. Accessed
May 28, 2022. https://www.aarp.org/health/brain-health/
global-council-on-brain-health/?cmp=RDRCT-GCBH_
Main_10_26_015.

CHAPTER 8:

Blennow, Kaj, David L. Brody, Patrick M. Kochanek, Har-
vey Levin, Ann McKee, Gerard M. Ribbers, Kristine Yaffe,
and Henrik Zetterberg. "Traumatic Brain Injuries." *Nature
Reviews Disease Primers* 2, no. 1 (2016). https://doi.org/10.1038/
nrdp.2016.84.

Laskas, Jeanne Marie. *Concussion*. London: Viking, 2016.

Leuzy, Antoine, Konstantinos Chiotis, Laetitia Lemoine, Per-
Göran Gillberg, Ove Almkvist, Elena Rodriguez-Vieitez, and
Agneta Nordberg. "Tau Pet Imaging in Neurodegenerative
Tauopathies—Still a Challenge." *Molecular Psychiatry* 24, no.
8 (2019): 1112–34. https://doi.org/10.1038/s41380-018-0342-8.

Mez, Jesse, Daniel H. Daneshvar, Patrick T. Kiernan, Bobak
Abdolmohammadi, Victor E. Alvarez, Bertrand R. Huber,
Michael L. Alosco, et al. "Clinicopathological Evaluation of
Chronic Traumatic Encephalopathy in Players of American
Football." *JAMA* 318, no. 4 (2017): 360. https://doi.org/10.1001/
jama.2017.8334.

"Natasha Richardson Died of Epidural Hematoma After Skiing
Accident." ABC News. ABC News Network. Accessed June
24, 2022. https://abcnews.go.com/Entertainment/Movies/
story?id=7119825&page=1.

Sacks, Oliver. *The Man Who Mistook His Wife for a Hat: And
Other Clinical Tales*. New York: Summit Books, 1985.

Salmond, Claire H., David K. Menon, Doris A. Chatfield, John
    D. Pickard, and Barbara J. Sahakian. "Cognitive Reserve as a
    Resilience Factor against Depression after Moderate/Severe
    Head Injury." *Journal of Neurotrauma* 23, no. 7 (2006): 1049–58.
    https://doi.org/10.1089/neu.2006.23.1049.

Urschel, John, and Louisa Thomas. *Mind and Matter: A Life in
    Math and Football.* New York: Penguin Books, 2020.

CHAPTER 9:

"Diagnosis." Watch Diagnosis | Netflix Official Site, August 16,
    2019. https://www.netflix.com/title/80201543.

Gilbert, Frederic, Eliza Goddard, John Noel Viaña, Adrian Car-
    ter, and Malcolm Horne. "I Miss Being Me: Phenomenological
    Effects of Deep Brain Stimulation." *AJOB Neuroscience* 8, no. 2
    (2017): 96–109. https://doi.org/10.1080/21507740.2017.1320319.

Gross, Robert A. "A Brief History of Epilepsy and Its Therapy in
    the Western Hemisphere." *Epilepsy Research* 12, no. 2 (1992):
    65–74. https://doi.org/10.1016/0920-1211(92)90028-r.

Jabr, Ferris. "The Man Who Controls Computers with His Mind."
    New York Times. The New York Times, May 12, 2022. https://
    www.nytimes.com/2022/05/12/magazine/brain-comput-
    er-interface.html.

Kenneally, Christine. "Do Brain Implants Change Your Iden-
    tity?" *The New Yorker,* April 15, 2021. https://www.newyorker.
    com/magazine/2021/04/26/do-brain-implants-change-your-
    identity.

Oxley, Tom. "Tom Oxley: A Brain Implant That Turns Your
    Thoughts into Text." Tom Oxley: A brain implant that turns
    your thoughts into text | TED Talk. June 2022. Accessed June
    24, 2022. https://www.ted.com/talks/tom_oxley_a_brain_
    implant_that_turns_your_thoughts_into_text.

Restak, Richard M. *Mysteries of the Mind*. Washington, DC: National Geographic, 2000.

Sacks, Oliver. *An Anthropologist on Mars: Seven Paradoxical Tales*. London: Picador, 1995.

Sanders, Lisa. "This Little Girl's Seizures Won't Stop. Her Parents Need Your Advice." *New York Times*. The New York Times, October 11, 2018. https://www.nytimes.com/interactive/2018/10/11/magazine/netflix-diagnosis-series-sadie.html.

"The RNS System." NeuroPace, Inc, March 22, 2022. https://www.neuropace.com/patients/neuropace-rns-system/.

Varadkar, Sophia, Christian G. Bien, Carol A. Kruse, Frances E. Jensen, Jan Bauer, Carlos A. Pardo, Angela Vincent, Gary W. Mathern, and J. Helen Cross. "Rasmussen's Encephalitis: Clinical Features, Pathobiology, and Treatment Advances." *The Lancet Neurology* 13, no. 2 (2014): 195–205. https://doi.org/10.1016/s1474-4422(13)70260-6.

WFAA. "NeuroPace RNS: A Breakthrough Surgery in Curbing Epilepsy That Can Be Done in 1.5 Hours." YouTube. YouTube, September 25, 2018. https://www.youtube.com/watch?v=l3oHSkfQ_x4.

CONCLUSION:

Gawande, Atul. *The Checklist Manifesto*. London: Profile Books Ltd, 2011.

9 798888 504 538 4